"When one of the Lord's most gifted disciples writes a book about His special prayer, that result is a spiritual treasure."

Dr. Bruce Larson, author, co-pastor of Crystal Cathedral

"Inner Wholeness through the Lord's Prayer is a prescription for life. Rita shares how modern man with all his problems can receive 'bread for today,' the Word of God from heaven. She shows how man searches in vain through multiple earthly avenues for peace and healing, while the life of God's Spirit is closer than His breathing.

"Rita's teachings concerning wholeness are true and anchored in God's Word. This book is good medicine; take the words in liberal doses for the healing of body and soul, no matter what your diagnosis may be. Enjoy and be made whole!"

William Standish Reed, M.D., surgeon and president of the Christian Medical Foundation

"While many works on the Lord's Prayer have helped meet the longing of our hearts, 'Lord, teach us to pray,' Rita's personal creative reflection has brought a wealth of refreshing insights for the wholeness of wounded hearts. Her 'maximized approach' and the study guide are particularly helpful. I happily recommend the book *Inner Wholeness through the Lord's Prayer* to a wide readership and thorough study in the Church."

The Rt. Rev. Dr. Moses Tay, Bishop of Singapore

D0059593

Other books by Rita Bennett

I'm Glad You Asked That!
Emotionally Free
How to Pray for Inner Healing for Yourself and Others
Making Peace with Your Inner Child

Co-authored with Dennis Bennett

The Holy Spirit and You
Trinity of Man

INNER WHOLENESS
THROUGH
THE LORD'S PRAYER

Rita Bennett

Published by
 chosen books

FLEMING H. REVELL COMPANY
TARRYTOWN, NEW YORK

The accounts in this book are factual; however, to protect confidentiality, some of the names of people and identifying details have been changed.

Some of the material in this book is quoted or revised from articles written by Rita Bennett for *The Morning Watch,* newsletter of the Christian Renewal Association, P.O. Box 576, Edmonds, WA, 98020 and later compiled into a booklet, *Inner Wholeness through the Lord's Prayer,* copyright © 1989 by Rita Bennett, and published by Christian Renewal Association. Permission has been given by the publisher to use this material.

Unless otherwise identified, all Scripture quotations are from the New King James Version. Copyright © 1979, 1980, 1982 Thomas Nelson, Inc., Publishers.

Scripture quotations identified KJV are from the King James Version of the Bible.

Old Testament Scripture quotations identified AMPLIFIED are taken from The Amplified Bible. Old Testament copyright © 1965, 1987 by The Zondervan Corporation. Used by permission.

New Testament Scripture quotations identified AMPLIFIED are from the Amplified New Testament, copyright © The Lockman Foundation 1954–1958, and are used by permission.

Scripture quotations identified GNB are from the Good News Bible–Old Testament copyright © American Bible Society, 1976; New Testament copyright © American Bible Society 1966, 1971, 1976.

Verses marked TLB are taken from The Living Bible, copyright © 1971 by Tyndale House Publishers, Wheaton, Ill. Used by permission.

Scripture quotations identified NASB are from the New American Standard Bible, copyright © The Lockman Foundation 1960, 1962, 1963, 1968, 1971, 1972, 1973, 1975, 1977.

Scripture texts identified NIV are from the Holy Bible, New International Version, copyright © 1973, 1978, 1984 International Bible Society. Used by permission of Zondervan Bible Publishers.

The Scripture quotations contained herein identified RSV are from the Revised Standard Version of the Bible, copyright © 1946, 1952, 1971 by the Division of Christian Education of the National Council of the Churches of Christ in the United States of America, and are used by permission. All rights reserved.

Italics and bracketed material are added by the author for emphasis.

The rendering of the Lord's Prayer the author used for chapter titles and throughout the book was based on the following translations: The Revised English Bible, The Book of Common Prayer, 1976, and the New King James Version, as well as the commentaries listed in this book.

Library of Congress Cataloging in Publication Data

Bennet, Rita.
    Inner wholeness through the Lord's prayer / Rita Bennett.
        p.   cm.
    ISBN 0-8007-9176-2
    1. Lord's prayer—Meditations.   2. Lord's prayer—Commentaries.
    I. Title.
    BV230.B46   1991
    242'.722—dc20   90-19826
                                                                        CIP

A Chosen Book
Copyright © 1991 by Rita Bennett
Chosen Books are published by
Fleming H. Revell Company
Publishers
Tarrytown, New York
Printed in the United States of America

This book is dedicated to my beloved husband,
Dennis Joseph Bennett,
one faithful to God and to his calling,
and faithful to me
for these 24 years of marriage.

Acknowledgments

First, great thanks go to my husband, Dennis, who walked through this book with me, copy editing, sharing his knowledge of Greek, giving me theological counsel and praying with me as we went along. We got our heads together for discussion on many fine points throughout the writing of this book.

Thanks go to our fellowship group that meets with us on a biweekly basis, and that has supported me in prayer through this project. The regulars are: Diane Durall, Beth Hubbard, Dave and Todd Olson, Jeff Thomas, Anita Zinter—not forgetting Dana Thompson who is currently on the field in Japan!

My deep appreciation goes to Don and Marlene Ostrom for the use of their condominium on Maui. Those two weeks got this book off to a good start.

Many thanks go to Mabel Whittaker who transcribed cassette tapes of classes I have given on the Lord's Prayer to help remind me of past spontaneous ideas that came as I taught.

Much appreciation goes to Janet Koether who has done indexing for me in the past and was willing to do this exacting task once again.

Thanks go to Ann McMath for her expert and insightful editing, and to Richard Herkes and Jane Campbell who encouraged me to write this book.

And last but not least my gratitude goes to Marilyn Speare, our new friend and fellow worker in the Christian Renewal ministry. She joined us the spring of '90 and has kept things running smoothly while I've been busy writing.

Ad majorem Dei gloriam!

Contents

9

Contents

Contents

Contents

14
Intercessory Prayer **169**

Meditate on His Word • Think Deeply About God's Love and Presence • Be An Intercessor • Give Thanks and Praise • Praying the Lord's Prayer for Someone Else • Be Still and Listen • A Closing Word

PART 2

15
How to Use This Study Guide **183**

16
Study Guide **186**

Preface

Why another book on the Lord's Prayer? Because we haven't yet learned its value in our lives. Because we need the inner wholeness it can bring. Because we haven't done what Jesus told us to. Because God's Kingdom hasn't yet come *in its fullness* and there's more work to be done.

Until God's Kingdom has fully come to earth, the Lord's Prayer is needed. It must not be devalued, diluted, debunked, diminished or divested of its power. It is a prayer for here and now; it won't be needed in heaven.

God wants to unlock for you the hidden treasure in the Lord's Prayer. You will be given gifts as you pray. You will find new ideas coming to you and strong impressions of action you should take to make this world a better place. You will receive greater protection over your thought life. As you live and pray the Lord's Prayer, you'll find you're living more in tune with God and will be surprised at the missions He'll be free to send you on. You will become more whole, and others will notice. They will ask for your counsel and prayer. Doors will open for you to increase your witness in the world.

So get ready for excitement and adventure in this most beneficial undertaking, praying . . . Jesus' way.

Part 1

1
Praying the Lord's Prayer "to the Max"

One of the most important things anyone can do is pray. Yet in your busy world it's probably one of the things you do least. How do I know? Because that's been my experience, too. Life is full of demands, just like so many eager little puppies yelping for attention.

Alphonsus Liguori, eighteenth-century bishop, said, "If I had only one sermon to preach, I would preach it on prayer."[1]

That's quite a statement. I wonder how many people, ministers and laypersons alike, would agree with it. I wonder something else, too: If we had more sermons on prayer and classes on how to do it effectively, wouldn't this world be a different kind of place?

Think for a moment: Why are we here on the face of the earth anyway? The Bible reveals that we are here to meet God personally and to grow in friendship with Him. How do we go about it?

In a way, it's a lot like marriage. It's all-important to meet the person you want to marry, but if you never spend time together deepening your relationship you will not develop the intimacy needed for a lifetime commitment and will not discover the joy marriage can give. Similarly, we must spend time in prayer in order to get to know God—Father, Son and Holy Spirit.

Out of this comes everything else: We know God's will and guidance, His wisdom and knowledge; we learn how to enter into thanksgiving, praise and worship; we are drawn to reflection or meditation; we find our own needs being met and learn how to intercede for others.

Prayer is mentioned 545 times in the Bible in various ways; we can have no doubt about its importance. We can also think of various definitions. A basic one is: communicating with God for fellowship, protection and direction to carry out His will. Prayer is you talking to God and God talking to you. It is speaking to God, tuning your heart to His and thus speaking into existence what He wants to happen; it's being His voice in a sea of confusion. Prayer is also listening to God, receiving His directions so we will say and do the right things.

The benefits of this communication are many, but one is especially meaningful for people living in a hurting world: Prayer is the way to inner wholeness, to inner peace. The closer you draw to God, the closer you will feel His healing arms around you. Prayer becomes vital. It is, in fact, the breath of the Christian life. It makes you sensitive to the whispers of the Holy Spirit. Through it you can be changed, and you can help change the world for good.

Who is going to teach you this most important of activities? Why not go to Jesus Christ, the One through whom the Father created all things?[2] Why not go to the Manufacturer Himself and to His own words, the words printers have colored in red? The

Gospel accounts preserve what He wants you to know. In fact, His words are pivotal to understanding all other words in the Bible. And we don't have to read very far to see how important prayer was to Him.

This leads naturally to the one specific prayer Jesus Christ taught His disciples to pray. It is best known as the Lord's Prayer, or the "Our Father," and is found twice in the Gospel records: Matthew 6:9–13 and Luke 11:2–4. I will be using the prayer as it was recorded by Matthew because it is the better known and includes the familiar doxology at the end.[3]

Over the centuries, this prayer has not lost any of its impact. To be sure, our reverence for it has grown. "In the early Church in the days of persecution," said the late Dr. Massey Shepherd, "the Lord's Prayer, like the Creed, was one of the mysteries that were not to be divulged to the unbaptized, so that it was only said in the company of the faithful, who could be 'bold' to say it without fear of its being betrayed to unworthy ears."[4] He said further that its public use in the Church can be traced back to the fourth century.

Jesus' powerful prayer has been translated into more languages than any other prayer. Undoubtedly more books have been written on it than any other religious topic, as time and again throughout history Christians of all branches of the Church have rediscovered Jesus' prayer and have shared their freshly inspired thoughts with the rest of us.

The Rev. Dr. Alfred Plummer, writing in James Hastings' *Dictionary of the Bible,* says, "Any one, of any race or age or condition, who believes in God, can use the Lord's Prayer, and use it just in proportion to his belief. A peasant child can understand enough of it to make it the expression of his daily needs. The ripest scholar, philosopher, and saint cannot exhaust all its possibilities of meaning. In a few minutes it may be committed to memory; but it is the work of a lifetime to learn it by heart. A

Christian's knowledge of the import of it grows with his spiritual experience. The prayer is at once a form, a summary, and a pattern."[5]

The Lord's Prayer is all-inclusive. Everything is there. All the basic steps of inner healing and wholeness are there. Faith in God and His presence. Bringing the Kingdom into our lives on this earth. Praying in God's will. Being forgiven and forgiving. Guidance and provision. Deliverance from evil. It shows an approachable, unconditionally loving God. There is an omnipresence about the prayer itself in that it gives us a vision of the past and present and things to come.

Jesus said that those who pray His prayer, taking time alone with it and God, will be rewarded by His Father. You will know those rewards and experience them even while you read on and pray your way through *Inner Wholeness through the Lord's Prayer*. As you read and pray, your fellowship with God will grow, and you will experience healing, particularly for your emotions and memories. This often opens the way for other healings, including physical ones.

Helping you to understand and use this prayer in depth and to receive its healing gifts is the main purpose of this book. First, a couple of general points about how it should be prayed.

Maximize or Minimize?

When we pray the Lord's Prayer we need to maximize it, not minimize it as is often done. What does it mean to minimize it? That's when it's spoken simply by rote, said almost mindlessly, in a church service perhaps with the person's mind on what she plans to serve for lunch, something like this:

"Our Father"

Let's see, when will the roast be ready?

'which art in heaven,"

20

It was an eight-pound roast. I put it on at nine-thirty and it's a bit after eleven now.

"Hallowed be thy name."

At twenty minutes a pound, it should be ready at 12:10.

"Thy kingdom come."

I wonder how many of their six children Jim and Betty will bring with them?

"Thy will be done"

Jack and Ella are coming alone.

"in earth as it is in heaven."

One should allow half a pound of meat per person—unless they're extra-big eaters.

"Give us this day our daily bread."

With Dave and myself the roast should feed sixteen people, and we'll only have twelve at the most.

"And forgive us our trespasses."

Oh, yes, Jack's a vegetarian. That leaves eleven.

"As we forgive those who trespass against us."

The salad is ready, but I've still got to peel and cook the potatoes.

"And lead us not into temptation,"

Then I'll need a vegetable—a green one, maybe broccoli.

"But deliver us from evil:"

Or a yellow one, butternut squash.

"For thine is the kingdom,"

We were always taught there should be a green and a yellow vegetable with our meals.

"And the power, and the glory,"

We'll have both!

"For ever and ever."

The rolls will need a quick warm-up in the oven.

"Amen."[6]

For dessert, ice cream and cookies.

Minister to congregation: "Please stand."

Church member: *It's funny, but I always feel so much better after saying the Lord's Prayer!*

Sound familiar? I'm sure you non-cooks could give renditions of planning your afternoon's work, sports activity or visit with friends!

Maximizing the Lord's Prayer, on the other hand, means savoring, chewing, absorbing the life-giving nourishment from its ingredients. Taking time with them and with Him. Letting His words make an impact on you. Allowing God time to speak to you personally. In this hour. In this day. For this generation. It means letting His prayer become a part of you, and you a part of it. That's using the Lord's Prayer to its fullest.

Verbatim or Reflective Prayer?

In Matthew's account, Jesus taught His disciples this prayer just after warning them not to use meaningless repetitions. The last thing Jesus wants you (and me) to do is to use the model prayer He gave us as a meaningless repetition! Yet you've heard it prayed that way, and undoubtedly have done so yourself. I admit that, like the woman planning the dinner, I have. It's easy to let our minds wander when repeating those well-known words, even though we know their vital importance.

We do often use Jesus' words—66 in number in the King James Version—as a prayer in church, and this is good. Praying corporately offers some real benefits and in giving us this prayer Jesus sanctioned such use. Jesus employed plural pronouns in the prayer to remind His hearers and us of the importance of seeing ourselves as one Body in Him.

But He obviously did not want it only to be repeated verbatim.

He gave it especially as a pattern for reflective, personalized praying. Scripture bears this out. "After this manner therefore pray," states the King James Version of Jesus' introduction to the prayer. "Pray along these lines," says The Living Bible.

For some years now I've discovered the satisfaction of using the Lord's Prayer reflectively—that is, as a *prayer outline*. As time and inspiration allow, I can pray it in ten or fifteen minutes, or an hour, or longer, using it in conjunction with other kinds of prayer, especially when I have unusual needs. At the conclusion of this book I'll share how personal prayers for others can be a natural follow-up to the Lord's Prayer.

Some churches believe it should be used privately for a certain amount of time daily, others use it every Sunday; some use it in every important service, others use it only when so inspired; some use it repetitively as a cleansing agent, and still others don't use it at all, believing it passé.[7]

It's true the Lord's Prayer has been an important feature of Christian worship from very early times, but in such a setting there is little time to pray it reflectively. Still, I think we would benefit from a brief reflective form used occasionally in church just as the Ten Commandments are. If we pray it only verbatim, we lose its full value.

Why did Jesus precede His prayer with the words "When you pray, go into your room, close the door and pray to your Father" (Matthew 6:6, NIV)? Here He is emphasizing the importance of individual prayer, which is vital in developing a personal relationship with God; certainly He wanted His disciples to take time with, to reflect on, the prayer He was about to give them. And He wants us, also being His disciples, to use this prayer in the way He knew it would be most beneficial.

Praying the Lord's Prayer reflectively is a means whereby a new Christian, or an old one, can know how to pray and what to pray about, and know he is praying in the will of God. It's a kind of checklist.

I remember a couple of years ago when Gary, a member of our church, requested that we have an all-night prayer vigil for a number of people who were seriously ill. (A very good idea, by the way.) Each person who wanted to participate selected a half-hour around the clock. When we met the following evening to share our experiences, quite a few people said, "After I offered the people on the list to God, I didn't know what else to do. So I did it over again, several times. It's amazing how slowly a half-hour goes by when you're sitting in a church praying alone!" Maybe you've had a similar experience. A prayer vigil based on using the Lord's Prayer reflectively and followed by intercessions would fill those hours powerfully.

The Reflective Lord's Prayer Made Easy

Let me confess right away that I don't pray the Lord's Prayer a half-hour every day without fail; sometimes it's fifteen minutes, sometimes thirty minutes and sometimes an hour. At times I've missed praying it at all. I don't believe in painting myself into a corner, even if it's a *prayer* corner! But my intention is to pray His prayer, to speak His desires into effect, as a part of my daily life. And I find that after you've walked through the Lord's Prayer reflectively, and maximized it to some extent, then on the occasions when you do pray it verbatim, it will have more significance.

It's fun to pray the Lord's Prayer reflectively in different places and see how creatively the Holy Spirit guides you. Vacationing on Maui in 1989, I reflected on His prayer while snorkeling in the beautiful blue ocean! It went something like this:

Our Father, Abba, Daddy, I love You. Father of the depths as well as the heights. Father who, through Your Son, divided the great land mass from the waters, and fashioned the world beneath the sea and all that live in it—such as these beautiful tropical fish swimming here with their blues and greens, their yellow and red rainbow hues.

Who is in heaven, and also on earth, You are omnipresent. You came down to earth through Your Son in a special way, to rescue us from drowning in our own sin.

Holy is Your name. By Your name all things, all creatures above and below the sea, exist. I reverence Your name. I will keep it holy.

Your Kingdom come. May human beings reverence Your creation and stop poisoning and polluting the waters, contaminating them and killing the whales, the fish, the ducks, the seagulls and others of Your creatures.

Your will be done. May we help clean up Your oceans, rivers, lakes and the air we breathe, that I'm breathing now through this snorkel.

On earth as it is in heaven. May we stop making money our god—messing up and destroying this earth for material gains. May our air and water be purified as they are in heaven. Show me what I can do to help, even in choices in my own home and city.

Give us today our daily bread. Thank You for nourishment from the sea. Your own Son was a fisherman, and chose most of His twelve disciples from those who made their living from the fish of the sea. Now we have to kill fish to live. How great it will be one day in Your fulfilled Kingdom where we won't need to kill any creature in order to live!

Forgive us our sins. If we humans take more than our quota of fish or crabs or other sea creatures and so deplete the necessary supply, or cause an imbalance in nature, please forgive us. If we've helped to cause the sea mammals to give up hope—washing up on the seashore to die—please forgive us. Forgive us for polluting the oceans of the world with oil spills; give us creative ideas on how to stop this as well as delivering the oil to those who need it.

As we forgive those who have sinned against us. I do forgive all others who have done these things. Please help me and those in authority find ways to stop the offenses against nature, until the offenders become wise enough to stop themselves.

And lead us not into temptation. Show us the way to live simply in harmony with nature, the water, air, ozone layer, land, flowers, trees, animals on land and in the sea. Help us not be so self-centered that we forget those generations yet to be born.

But deliver us from evil and the evil one. Help us not get our directions from the destroyer but from our Creator. Show us how to make a firm but loving stand against those who maim and kill for the love of money. Deliver us from destructive experimenters with nature.

For Yours is the Kingdom. Help us not be ashamed of the world's condition when Your Son comes back to earth.

And the power. Thanks for sharing some of Your power to help me stand tall for You and Your world.

And the glory, forever. The glorious array of colors and sizes of fishes and other sea life around the reefs; the world that often goes unseen; the blues, greens, grays of the water. But all these wonders are not as glorious as the God, Father, Son and Holy Spirit, who designed and created them all!

Amen. So be it!

The position of your body isn't important to God when you're praying. Whether you're flat on your back, standing on your head or swimming makes no difference to Him. You can pray it aloud or with your mouth closed. (I advise you to do the latter when swimming!)

You can pray the Lord's Prayer reflectively when waiting for a family member or friend to shop in a grocery store or clothing store, while jogging, relaxing in a jacuzzi or sauna, waiting at a dentist's or optometrist's office, on a bus or plane. Anytime you have five minutes or more with nothing to do. If you get interrupted, just continue when you're free. Anytime you're doing something that doesn't take much concentration, you can pray this prayer.

Todd Olson, a young adult friend, was a little nervous when he landed a job that could have made such demands on his time as to hinder his spiritual walk. This is especially understandable since he's nearly completed his first year of sobriety. I said, "Todd, you could take a 'Lord's Prayer break' right on the job." He chuckled at the idea, and when I checked with him later he said he's finding it extremely helpful. You can do this, too, using a daily coffee break for prayer.

How to Use this Book "to the Max"

There are various ways to use this book effectively. Ideally you could read it once for each way given.

1. Read through the chapters sequentially to get an overview of the teaching. Reflect on the words and apply them to your life. Avoid applying them to anyone other than yourself at first. As you go along, pray the prayers given and wait attentively. Give the Holy Spirit a chance to work in your soul.

2. Read in the silence of your spirit; let Jesus' prayer reveal its inner depths to you, beyond words. Let healing insights come to you to heal your soul: the inner child, teen or adult self. Keep a

notebook, a journal, and write down what the Lord says to you. As you read the reflective prayers found at the ends of the chapters, write down *your own* special reflections.

3. Skim the book at one sitting, this time paying special attention to the reflective prayers given at the end of each section. Close your eyes, letting these and the prayers you've written come back to you. Try to find time daily for this healing meditation.

4. Look at the Lord's Prayer in the light of helping others. Become an intercessor for their healing, as you go on to spend time in the teachings of the concluding chapter. Praying His prayer reflectively will help to make you a clear vessel through whom God can work. Do this intercessory work for yourself and for others as God directs you.

5. Lead your prayer group or church group in praying this prayer together in a brief reflective form. And/or have them pray for one another in groups of two. (See the section "Praying the Lord's Prayer for Someone Else.") You can use this book to teach in your congregation or home, and lead small groups through the study guide provided at the book's conclusion. Here they can share their thoughts with one another. This is a great way to build God's Kingdom.

Here are three ways you can pray the Lord's Prayer:

Verbatim: that is, exactly as it's written, using it by yourself or with others in a group, such as in church.

Reflectively: that is, verbatim though personalized by taking time to reflect on His words and meanings for periods of time. Here, too, let God's presence release you from stress.

Maximized: that is, reflectively and personalized. Taking time to let God speak to you. Being open to inner wholeness. Keeping a journal. Going on into intercessory prayer, and perhaps teaching what you've learned to others.

You will carry the prayer with you—in you. It will become part of you. Allow its meaning to infuse everything you do—your talking, your thinking, your feeling, your responding. Let it speak to your spirit and to the heart of your soul, not only to your intellect. Go to sleep praying it at night and let it work in your subconscious all night long. This is praying the Lord's Prayer reflectively, and to the maximum.

I'm thankful I can share some of the ways this greatest of prayers has inspired me. I wouldn't want to be without it! The Lord's Prayer is the master and foundation for prayers of inner wholeness—as well as for all prayer—composed by the Master Healer Himself. Please join me in exploring its riches.

2
Our Father

Think of the most loving and forgiving, gentle yet strong, considerate and affirming, brilliant yet humble, unselfish and courageous father imaginable. Now multiply that a million times over and you'll begin to have an inkling of what your heavenly Father is like.

The clearest picture the Bible shows of our heavenly Father is in the well-known story of the Prodigal Son and the forgiving, compassionate father (Luke 15:11–32). Jesus left this parable for us, and He knew then and has certainly known from all eternity what His Father is like!

It's a story of unconditional love. In it a trusting father allows his determined younger son to leave home with his full inheritance, knowing that his son's immaturity and faulty decision-making will get him into trouble.

This is the challenge all parents experience. Though we'd like to protect our children and keep them from making major mistakes, holding onto them can have even more damaging results than letting them go. The Prodigal's father then was also a wise father.

Yet he never gave up on his son, but would walk down the desert roads, or to the post delivery location or to the neighbors' homes hoping and praying for word from his beloved child. After waiting many long months, perhaps years, one day he saw his defeated son, ragged and dusty, walking slowly toward home.

The father *ran* to meet his repentant son, threw his arms around him with tears of joy. The humbled son didn't expect to come back under his roof but only hoped to be as one of the servants. The generous father would have none of that, but welcomed his son back into full status. Not only this; the father ordered a celebration to share his joy with others. And for the event the father had his son dressed in the best robe with sandals for his feet and even a special ring for his finger, perhaps the father's very own. The story that father and son had to tell that night would have been one worth hearing!

This amazing person was a noncontrolling parent—that is, one who allows his child to think, not simply act mechanically. He permitted his son, who was of age, to try his wings and then allowed him to come home without laying a shame trip on him. This son had a safe place to fail, to fall and to get up again. In such a healing atmosphere the son would feel secure enough to try again and again, each time with more wisdom than before, until one day he would become the same kind of man his father was.

This vignette Jesus gave of a loving father shows us the kind of Person we talk to when we pray, "Our Father"! Old Testament leaders like Moses and David, prophets like Isaiah, Jeremiah and Hosea, gave us little glimpses of God. From them we can glean much inspiration; yet none of them, including the New Testament writers, had a complete picture of Him. Paul says we all, including himself and those who came before him, see as though peering through a glass darkly illuminated (1 Corinthians 13:12). *Jesus is the only One who didn't.* So if you want to see the Father you must look through Jesus' eyes; you do this by reading His words, and through praying.

One of the main reasons Jesus came to earth was to reveal His Father. The disciples wanted to know what His Father was like, just as you and I do. Philip, acting as spokesman for the Twelve, pressed Him, "Show us the Father." Jesus' response was, "Have I been with you so long, and yet you have not known Me, Philip? He who has seen Me has seen the Father" (John 14:8–9).

Here Jesus explains He is just like His Father in everything—purpose, thought, word and deed. If you know what Jesus is like, then you know what His Father in heaven is like. Hebrews 1:3 says He is the "express image" of the Father. It's vital to see that Jesus is exactly like His Father, because it makes the Father so much more approachable and understandable to us.

My husband, Dennis, pointed this out one day: "With a healthy human father-son relationship, you may say, 'That boy is the very image of his dad!', and that means when you meet one you'll have a good idea what the other will be like. But Jesus is not just *like* His Father; He is one with the Father and the Holy Spirit in a way that goes beyond our understanding. The Three are One, and yet They are each separate Persons. The relationship of Jesus with the Father is infinitely more than any human father and son could show, but it is not *less* than that."

32

An Unhealthy Fear of God

Drawing a parallel between earthly fathers and our heavenly Father may not always be a positive association. Before we go any further I want to speak briefly to those of you who may find yourself getting stuck on these first two words of the Lord's Prayer. Here's a truth crucial for your understanding. You must be able to distinguish between your earthly father and your heavenly Father when thinking of God. Unless you've been healed from hurtful childhood emotions and memories, *you will see God as you experienced your earthly father.*

If your human father was gone nearly all the time, you may feel God is unavailable to you. If he was verbally, physically or sexually abusive, you will be fearful of and unable to trust God and will want to keep a safe distance from Him. If he never spent time with you or affirmed you, you may feel of little worth. Many atheists and agnostics had poor fathers or father figures, or perhaps religious leaders who represented God to them may have disillusioned them; worse yet, perhaps both occurred. Likewise a minister's child with a harmful father relationship will have a double problem with God. After all, Dad speaks for God from the pulpit, so how can he be wrong at home?

I want to tell you about a young woman I'll call Jill. She was so fearful of God that when she went to church she'd actually tremble throughout the service. As a child and young adult she saw a lot of physical and verbal fighting between her mother and father. They divorced and her mother remarried. When her stepfather began pursuing Jill romantically there was another divorce. At the churches she attended God was usually portrayed as anything but kind. She began, finally, to attend church with some trustworthy friends and learned God wasn't erratic but unconditionally loving. As she experienced that love through her friends and their prayers, her healing began and the trembling ceased.

Jill is certainly not alone in her struggle. There is no way to estimate the vast numbers of people hurt by oppressive fathers, or the depths of those hurts, but I find this quote from the chaplain of the Danvers (Massachusetts) State Mental Hospital extraordinarily revealing: "I've found I can't use the Lord's Prayer with patients during worship service, because so many of them have emotionally unhealthy fathers or father figures. To use this prayer would cause the patients to have trouble relating to God at all."[1]

What a commentary on the father-Father relationship! And what a loss to such a needy group of people!

John DeWitt, chaplain for the King County Correctional Facility, Seattle, says, "In my twelve years of experience in the jail ministry in counseling and dealing with men eighteen years old and above, I find that eighty percent of these inmates have had poor father relationships. For the women it's a little better, about sixty percent."

This isn't the way it was meant to be. Scripture says that fathers are the glory of their children (Proverbs 17:6).[2] That is, fathers are supposed to be such good and loving examples that their children will be drawn to God. Fathers then have a double role to play. While boys get masculine identity through a father, both boys and girls get a primary picture of how they view God from him. In this way, then, a father may be the glory of his children, or the shame.

The importance of the mother's role is obvious because of her closeness to her child throughout pregnancy and her continued closeness during infancy and childhood. A child continues to get his feelings and emotional responses (good or bad) primarily from his mother. But the point, for our purposes, is that the father's role, which is often underestimated, is vital to a child's perception of God.

So a word to you fathers (and you mothers, too): Draw your children to God rather than drive them away from Him. Perhaps you need healing in your own lives. Perhaps other factors, known and unknown, have caused your child's wounding. Whatever the case, you'll be better equipped to pray with him or her if you've been healed yourself.

If your children are grown you may think it's too late to make a difference. This is not necessarily so. It's amazing what a letter, a call, a prayer, an "I'm sorry" can do to begin healing relationships. Gaining inner wholeness can enable you to forgive yourself and others, and give you new and creative ideas to bring about reconciliation.

While Dennis and I were teaching a seminar in a church in the San Francisco Bay area, a couple requested healing prayer for their wandering son who had left home and had not contacted them for nearly a year. Those seeking prayer had gathered in a number of small groups; in theirs, they prayed for forgiveness for their own mistakes, and forgave their son for his. They sobbed their way through several hours of prayer that Saturday night. The very next morning as they sat in church, to their joy and amazement their son walked in and sat down beside them! The result of prayer is awesome, isn't it?

If you have trouble seeing God as a loving Father, just take my word for now that He is, and keep on reading. Much healing will come as you go along.

It may also help to know that Jesus has spoken these words to people while they were praying: *I will be as a father to you.* He didn't say He would be the Father, but that He would be "as a father." In other words, it's O.K. for now if you don't relate as well to the Father as to the Son; eventually you will. Let Jesus be *as a father* to you, and He will bring you to the Father Himself. He's done that for many people, including those of us who have had positive or semi-positive relationships with our earthly fathers. Just take hold of Jesus' hand.

Jesus has often "fathered" me through difficult times. Then one day, while I was listening to the choir at St. Alban's Church, I realized that Jesus was now more in the role of Brother, and I was relating more personally to my Father, God. Jesus over the years had gently revealed Him to me. Matthew 11:27 says, "All things have been delivered to Me by My Father, and no one knows the Son except the Father. Nor does anyone know the Father except the Son, and he to whom the Son wills to reveal Him."

If you simply can't continue with the Lord's Prayer at this time, you need what James 5:14 teaches. Share your problems with a team of two or three people who are knowledgeable about and effective in prayer. Receive ministry until your vision of God changes. Attend a Christ-centered church where the love of God is stressed. Read books on soul or inner healing prayer.[3] God will move all heaven to assist you in your quest for healing as you take even a small step in this direction.

The First to Call Him "Abba, Father"

Jesus is eager to share His Father with you. He is inexpressibly happy that you can have His Father for your Father. How do I know this? Because of what He has said. After Jesus' death and resurrection, the apostle John records that Mary Magdalene was the first person to see Him. I believe Jesus was smiling and perhaps lifting His hands with joy when He commissioned her, "Go to My brethren, and say to them, 'I ascend *to My Father and your Father,* and My God and your God" (John 20:17, NASB). These were His first recorded words after His resurrection, and they were unfathomably important. His great work was accomplished! The way had been opened for human beings to be adopted into the heavenly Father's family. Jesus could have brothers and sisters now, and the Father could have many children through His only begotten Son.

Hebrew and Aramaic children call their fathers "Abba," which, like "Papa," denotes affection and tenderness. "Father" can seem quite formal, whereas "Papa" or "Daddy" is personal. Jesus is the first person I find in Scripture who addresses God the Father in this way, clearly showing His intimate relationship with Him.[4] He called out, "Abba, Father" in the Garden of Gethsemane as He prayed for strength to lay down His life. "If it's possible," Jesus said, "let this cup pass from Me: nevertheless . . ." (see Mark 14:36). In other words, He had already made His decision and had "set His face like a flint" to do this act of unconditional love (see Isaiah 50:5–7; Luke 9:51). We know this also from the classic beauty of the chapter about the Good Shepherd in which He talks about giving His life: "No one takes it from me, but I lay it down of my own accord" (John 10:18, NIV; see also verses 11, 15).

Let's look at this idea for a moment because it is critically important to our understanding of the Father's love.

Some people look at Jesus' agony in the Garden this way: "He was trying to get out of giving His life, but His Father was determined to put Him on the cross where He would pay for the sins of the world."

That is not true! The Father, the Son and the Holy Spirit decided ahead of time together how to save this world from the power of Satan, after our first parents would give over their dominion through their willful disobedience to God, the effect of which—separation from God—has come down upon us all.

God could have said, "Let's forget this whole race of people. They're a mess. They started killing right away, and doing all manner of evil because of their fallen condition, and they are going to get worse and worse." God could have said, "Let's wipe 'em all out and forget it."

No, instead He said, "We love them, as bad as they are, and so We'll make opportunity for them to be rescued." That opportunity was made when Jesus laid down His life for us.

Dennis is sometimes given parables. I find them helpful and I want to share one with you:

"A father and his adult son are sitting on an isolated beach in the evening, looking at a heavy surf breaking over a rocky shore-line. They're great friends and they've had a good time together. Their conversation is interrupted abruptly by the cry of a swimmer caught in the stormy waves, obviously in serious trouble. Instantly, the son jumps to his feet and pulls off his jacket and shoes. The father springs to his feet, too, and at first reaches out to restrain his son, but then realizes he must let him go to the rescue. The son plunges into the boiling surf and, after a struggle, locates the swimmer and drags him to safety. But just as he does so, he himself is caught by a wave, dashed against the rocks and killed.

"The father did not want the son to risk his life, and is grief-stricken at his death, but both of them had known that the attempt had to be made to save the drowning man."

The great thing for us is that Jesus didn't just die; He rose from the dead. Still, I think this parable gives a helpful picture of what the Father and Son were really like in Their loving relationship, and how Jesus willingly chose to give His life for us on the cross.

I heard about a young man who was an actor in a Passion play, telling the story of Christ's life. He played the role of the Father in heaven, and as he watched Jesus being beaten and crucified, the young actor had such physical pain he thought his heart would break. I think our Father allowed him a little glimpse of His own

38

pain so he would realize how the Father suffered, too. If you've ever lost a child of your own through death, you will especially be able to identify with the Father's pain.

We know, further, that Jesus was not trying to get out of giving His life because He could actually have changed the scenario. Matthew reports that as Jesus was being arrested He told Peter to put away his sword because He could ask His Father for "twelve legions of angels" to rescue Him (Matthew 26:53, KJV). The New American Standard Bible says a legion equaled six thousand; so by this calculation twelve legions equaled 72,000 angels. In Isaiah 37:36 we find that one angel of the Lord in one night destroyed 185,000 of God's enemies.[5] If one angel accomplished that, 72,000 angels could kill 13,000,320,000 people (that's thirteen billion plus!). That's 8,000,128,000 more people than are presently on earth. So, 72,000 angels could easily wipe out the whole earth's present population. In fact, they could conquer two and a half times the earth's present population![6]

The point is that Jesus didn't seek a way of escape, though His Father would have immediately provided it at His Son's request. This statement to Peter shows Jesus wanted to make sure we wouldn't blame His Father for His death. Jesus' heart's desire and purpose for coming to earth was to complete the rescue of mankind, to restore us to the Father, by giving up His own life and fulfilling God's plan as revealed in Scripture (see Matthew 26:53–54; John 14:6).

He prayed that the cup of suffering might pass from Him not because He didn't want to die for you and me, but for two other reasons. First, Jesus who is God incarnate—without beginning, and without ending—had always been with His Father in loving fellowship. On the cross He had all the sins of mankind, beginning with Adam until the end of time, laid upon Himself. In those last three hours on the cross, darkness covered the earth as a portrayal of what was happening spiritually. Jesus was separated from his Father for the very first and only time. Why? Because sin separates from God the Father, and Jesus took the sins of the whole world upon Himself.

That's a lot of sins! All those sins were piled on Jesus Christ, and during His separation from the Father, *He experienced hell for the whole human race.* Hell is separation from God, the One who loves you most. Jesus experienced hell so that you don't ever have to. His sorrow at the thought of that separation was the main reason He said, "Let this cup pass from Me." But He gave His life for you, willingly. He chose to do that.

The second reason is that He was fully God but also fully man. That is, though He was and is without sin, yet while on earth He chose to live like us and experience the weakness of humanity. *It's hard to die.* Even though He knew He was born to die for us and His Spirit was willing, His soul and body still had a terrific battle against it.

Why do I tell this old and glorious story again? Because many people have heard it but heard it wrong, and they unknowingly promote an unloving picture of our Father, God. This keeps a lot of people away from the Father's house.

But Jesus shows us the Father's love time and again, love that allowed His Son to go, so that we might know God as "our Father."

A Second Cry of "Abba, Father"

Twice it's recorded that the apostle Paul called God "Abba." Paul had a true revelation of what Jesus has done for us when he said, "Because you are sons, God has sent forth the Spirit of His Son into your hearts, crying out, 'Abba, Father!' " (Galatians

4:6). By the power of the Holy Spirit, Jesus is still calling, "Abba, Father" through His brothers and sisters on earth, and He's helping you call to the Father also.

In order to truly say, "Our Father," you must be born from above, by receiving Jesus Christ into your life just as a little child. God the Son knocks at every heart's door, and at some point every human person needs to pray, "Come in, Lord Jesus." As you go on in the power of the Holy Spirit, you will find it even easier to say, "Father," and, "Abba, Daddy." Then as you seek help for the healing of hurts and relationships, you'll be drawn even closer to intimacy with Father and Son.

Again, Paul says to the Roman believers, and to all believers, "For you did not receive the spirit of bondage again to fear, but you received the Spirit of adoption by whom we cry out, 'Abba, Father' " (Romans 8:15).

Charles Laymon, editor of *The Interpreter's Bible Commentary,* says about this passage: "Here is a glimpse into the prayers of the earliest churches, still using the original Aramaic 'Abba' for Father. Prayer is connected with the activity of the Spirit again in vss. 26–27. It is the function of the Spirit to witness, i.e., to cause consciousness of the new and unique privilege of relation to God."[7]

When you have the Spirit of adoption, you've been adopted into God's family. Even if you didn't have a family of your own who wanted you, even if you were an adopted child, even if you were born with a feeling of rejection, God says, "My child, I've put you in My family now. You're adopted into My family."

So much is healed when we begin to concentrate on being in His family, no matter what our own personal family was or is like. We're in His family, and we can cry out to our Father whatever the need may be.

You Are Loved

You, having received God's Son, Jesus Christ, have a special place in God's heart that no one else can fill—only you. It has your name on it, Jeanne or Joan, Jack or John. Fill in the blank with whatever your name is. No one else can fill that place in God's heart other than you. He needs you as much as He needs anyone else in this world.

"What?" some people would say. "Why would God need me?" Well, He does! Just as an earthly parent needs a child after he's been born, so God needs you after you were born into His family. He loves you as much as He loves anyone else in this world. That's the way He is. That's the way He loves.

Wonderful things can happen as you pray, "Abba, Father."

You as an individual have a Father, and you can also rejoice in saying "our" Father corporately because He has a large and growing family composed of many on earth and those in heaven (Hebrews 2:10–17; 12:1–2). Let's pray "my Father," and then let's be inclusive and also say "our Father," as we acknowledge we're all in one family—the family of God.

This incredible Father loves you *even as He loves His Son,* Jesus Christ. I know this because in John 17:23 Jesus gives this revelation of His Father's love: "That the world may know and [definitely] recognize that You sent Me, and that You have loved them [even] as You have loved Me" (Amplified). Jesus says further that He will continue to reveal His Father and His love to us: "Righteous Father, though the world does not know you, I know you, and they know that you have sent me. I have made you known to them, and *will continue to make you known* in order that the love you have for me may be in them and that I myself may be in them" (John 17:25–26, NIV).

You would never hang your head and feel inferior if you could

42

always remember whose child you are! You are special to Him. He loves you unconditionally. Take some time to thank Him for the joy and privilege of calling Him "Abba, Father."

Prayer

"Our Father . . ."

Thank You, Lord Jesus Christ, for making it possible for Your Father to be my Father, too.

"Thank You, Father, for loving me, for never giving up on me. Thank You that You are always for me, that I am special to You.

[Repeat His name, "Father, my Father, Abba, Daddy, heavenly Father," until you know yourself to be in His presence. He loves you. Receive His love.]

Pause and reflect.

3
In Heaven

What is heaven like? Where is it located? In this day of space exploration with men walking on the moon, perhaps it isn't too fantastic for modern people, non-Christians as well as Christians, to contemplate a place in the universe called heaven. In past times epic poets like Milton and Dante tried to describe it. In modern times writers like C. S. Lewis have done so, too.

It's not surprising that there are hundreds of references to heaven in the Bible, starting at the beginning and going through to the end, but in Scripture as in our everyday speech, the word *heaven* can be used in different ways. It can refer to the visible sky, as "the heavens were covered with clouds." In the Bible it also can refer to a region sometimes called "the air," which does not mean the atmosphere, but a local spiritual realm where Satan and his forces make their headquarters. This is what Paul is talking about in Ephesians 6:12: "For we wrestle not against flesh and blood, but against . . . the rulers of the darkness of this world, against spiritual wickedness [actually wicked spirits] in heavenly places'' (KJV, see margin note).

In the Lord's Prayer, *heaven* is clearly referring to the heavenly home where God dwells. As *The New Bible Dictionary* puts it, it is ''the present abode of God and His angels, and the ultimate destination of His saints on earth.''[1]

The apostle John in the book of Revelation described his vision of the glorious City of God. It has a wall around it made of jasper (an opaque quartz of several colors of dark green). The City and the highway running through it are made of pure gold, ''like clear glass.'' Its twelve foundations are each adorned with a different kind of precious stone. The twelve gates of the City are made from twelve gigantic pearls. In the center of the City are God's throne and that of Jesus, the Lamb of God, encircled by a rainbow like an emerald; before the throne is a fountain of living water flowing into a sea of crystal, and a crystal-clear river of life surging out from the throne.

By this refreshing river grows the Tree of Life, which constantly bears twelve kinds of nourishing and delicious fruit. Its leaves are ''for the healing of the nations''; apparently even the leaves have healing properties in them which people need when they first arrive in heaven.[2] (See Revelation 4, 5, 21, 22.)

Perhaps no modern writer has done more than C. S. Lewis to illustrate in simple words and tales what these mysteries of heaven may be like. In the third of his famous Narnia stories, *The Voyage of the Dawn Treader,* he described the water at the ''end of the world.'' As the children and others in the story drank of this living water they responded in various ways: ''It is sweet. That's real water, that. I'm not sure that it isn't going to kill me. But it is the death I would have chosen.'' ''It—it's like light more than anything else.'' ''That is what it is . . . drinkable light.'' ''It's the loveliest thing I have ever tasted. . . . We shan't need to eat anything now." "And one by one everybody on board drank. And for a long time they were all silent. They felt almost too well and strong to bear it. . . ." Surely Lewis had in mind something like the "river of the water of life" that John saw (Revelation 22:1)!

And in *The Last Battle,* the concluding book of the series, Lewis pictures a marvelous tree, which reminds us of the Tree of Life that John describes in Revelation 22:2.

"What was the fruit like? Unfortunately, no one can describe a taste. All I can say is that, compared with those fruits, the freshest grapefruit you've ever eaten was dull, and the juiciest orange was dry, and the most melting pear was hard and woody, and the sweetest wild strawberry was sour. And there were no seeds or stones, and no wasps. If you had once eaten that fruit, all the nicest things in this world would taste like medicine after it. But I can't describe it. You can't find out what it is like unless you can get to that country and taste it for yourself."[3]

The book of Revelation records further that in the heavenly City there are no tears of sorrow, no more pain, no sickness, no more death. It's a place of singing and joy, love and praise. Jesus is the Light of it, and there is no night or limitation of time there (Revelation 21:4, 23; 22:5). Obviously John is using visionary language in trying to describe the indescribable, but that means the reality is not *less* than he is saying, but more!

In the much-loved words of John 14:2–3 Jesus tells His disciples that there are "many mansions" in His Father's house and that He will go to prepare a place for them. In Elizabethan times *mansion* meant a place to stay—a dwelling place, an abode. This is what the Greek word μονή means. It can also mean "a room," and so the usually helpful NIV translates this, "In my Father's house are many rooms," but that sounds to me like a motel! I prefer to think Jesus was talking about mansions in the sense of beautiful houses.

Glimpses of Heaven?

In recent years there has been increasing interest in the experiences of those who have died (or nearly so), gone to heaven or heaven's outskirts, and come back to describe it in various ways: "incredibly peaceful, filled with light, music and joy"; "a place that imparts a love for everyone—even the worst offenders on earth."

I've found these accounts inspiring, although I'm quite aware that we can't prove anything from them. Doctors, nurses and pastors, whose work brings them in touch with the dying, know that amazing and beautiful things can happen at this time.

My own father, when he was so near death that he could not speak or move, suddenly raised his arms in praise to the Lord! Although vital signs continued for a while after that, I believe this was the moment his spirit went to be with the Lord.

At an early morning men's breakfast class, a man in Dennis' congregation—a rather "macho," rugged type, not given to sentimentality—told Dennis he had dreamed about heaven the night before. He said, "At first it was a long distance away. Then I asked the Lord if I could see it up close and, when I did, it was so beautiful that I fainted, right in my dream!"

Crossing a Bridge to the Other Side

A friend of mine, Pam Johnstone, is a capable business-woman, vice president of a Seattle bank. She told me of an experience she had during surgery some years before when she was 23 and her husband, Brian, was in language school at a military base in Fort Ord, California.

She began to have severe stomach pains that could not be diagnosed. Pam seemed too young for a gall bladder attack, but Brian thought that might be the cause, since there was a hereditary weakness in her family. Subsequent tests did show a non-functioning gall bladder to be the problem.

Pam had been given heavy pain medication for some time before the surgery, and when she was put under anesthesia for the operation itself she went into a deeper than normal sleep. She told me: "I just wanted to die. I didn't want to feel the pain any longer. Childbirth with my first child was nothing compared to this pain. Besides, you know labor pains will end, and you know why you're in pain.

"Sometime during the surgery, or in the recovery room, I felt I had 'awakened' in another place other than the hospital or my home," she continued. "I guess I'd say I was aware of all my senses. I felt no pain, which was wonderful, and there was a nice cool breeze blowing on me like you feel when you're driving in the car with your window down. The temperature was perfect. There was a peace and an all-over comfort you could never ever imagine. There was a lightness and calmness that is hard to describe. I remember a bright light like sunlight on a sunny afternoon when you'd normally need sunglasses, light like the reflection that comes off a body of water.

"The next thing I remember was walking and looking around trying to figure out where I was. It was sort of like a green meadow. Walking was easy there; it was more like flowing than walking. I found myself at one end of a bridge that crossed over to the other side. I looked down in order to step up to a higher footpath going up to the bridge. When I stepped onto the bridge, there was someone ahead of me about halfway across. The light was shining behind the person, I thought coming from the garments, so I couldn't see who it was. I kept walking, trying to make out who the person was. Then as I walked further on the bridge, he (or she, I couldn't tell) put his hand onto the bridge rail in front of me to prevent my crossing over. Then I said, 'I want to cross over.' I put my hand on his to push it away, and I looked up at his face and still saw only a real bright light and couldn't make out the features of the person. I said again, 'I want to get to the other side.' A very soothing voice responded to me, 'It's not your time.'

"I said, 'I don't care what time it is. I'm not going to feel this kind of pain anymore!' He said, 'You will not feel this kind of pain anymore. You have to go back; you're still needed there.'

"The next thing I knew I heard Brian's voice calling me, 'Pam! Pam!' And when I awoke, I saw the doctor, nurses and my husband all standing around my bed. Then I said to Brian emphatically, 'What do you want!' They all seemed relieved and said I could go back to sleep. I wondered why they were trying so hard to wake me and then in the next breath telling me to go back to sleep!''

When Pam woke again, the doctor came in and told her that they had tried to awaken her all day. They thought she was going into a coma, which she might not have come out of. They had been ready to call her father (she was very close to him) to fly down from Seattle to see if his voice could rouse her.

She told the doctor about the kind of ''dream experience'' she had had while under anesthesia and asked him if he believed in a world beyond this. He told her that he was a Christian and believed she had had a near-death experience. He said, ''When you came back you had a presence, alertness and puzzled awareness that aren't normal for people coming out of a semi-coma.''

I asked Pam, ''How do you feel about death now?''

She said, "I've never been afraid of it, and that's even more true since my being so near dying. The only remorse I'd have would be from leaving my family and other loved ones behind. I can't explain it, but it's not something I fear."

Paul rejoices that for those who accept Jesus, death has lost its victory (1 Corinthians 15:55–57). We might pause to consider that the living are a minority group in comparison to the vast majority of those who have lived and died and made their final journey.[4]

When my dad died I found among his papers an anonymous verse written by a woman whose child had died:

> Think of stepping on the shore and finding it heaven;
> Of touching a hand, and finding it God's;
> Of breathing new air, and finding it celestial;
> Of walking in glory, and finding it love.

A Tunnel of Thousands of Rainbows

"Before Don Cesar Vallerotto's dead body hit the ground, his spirit was flying through space to the edge of the universe. In a matter of seconds, all thoughts of this world were gone. He found himself in front of a large, imposing door that opened of its own accord like an accordion. Stretching before him was a vast tunnel composed of thousands of gorgeously colored rainbows. He hurried inside."

Thus Phil Saint, freelance writer and evangelist in Argentina, wrote in *Christian Life* magazine of Vallerotto's death and return.[5] The Baptist pastor, now nicknamed Lazarus by his townspeople, and his wife had gone to the church secretary's home to try to help restore the power that had been cut off during a hailstorm. In the process of trying to repair the 220-volt lines, the full force of the electric current shot through his body. He fell to the ground and gave a long, drawn-out groan. He appeared to have died and his wife ran to call a doctor.

The article goes on: "Within five minutes two doctors were checking the inert corpse of the stocky, heavy-set preacher. His body had turned a blotched purple. . . .

"One of the doctors pulled Vallerotto's swallowed tongue back to a normal position. The stethoscope showed no heartbeat. With an air of finality, he turned to the crowd of neighbors who had come running from all directions.

" 'Don Cesar is dead.'

"Nevertheless for seven more minutes the doctors continued to check for life processes. There were none. So they carried the body to the manse. Doña Giovanna, suddenly widowed, began thinking of funeral preparations for her beloved companion of some 45 years.

"Vallerotto, meanwhile, began walking briskly along under the thousands of delicate rainbows. Glancing up, he saw a lovely sign which said in Spanish: 'Enter in at the narrow gate; for wide is the way that leads to destruction.' Breathing the invigorating air, and feeling younger and stronger than he ever had in his earthly existence, he came to where the tunnel opened out onto gently rolling fields. There were tall graceful trees, beautiful bushes and gorgeous flowers. Music, far more thrilling than anything he had ever heard in this world, floated on the heavenly breezes. Multitudes of angels surrounded him.

"Suddenly Vallerotto became aware of another Presence. He knew it was the Lord. His hair was white as snow; His long white robe, glowing with brilliant light, was circled with a golden girdle. For a moment Vallerotto was disturbed: The Lord had His arms outstretched as if blocking his way. Then He spoke:

" 'You will enter here, but not now.' His voice was warm and modulated. 'You must go back to earth. There is much for you to do there yet.'

"Suddenly the corpse opened its eyes! The onlookers surrounding the bed caught their breath! As his color came back, a smile lit up his face.

" 'How wonderful it is to die!' Vallerotto said clearly and strongly. 'Death in Christ is the beginning of a life filled with light, music, joy and love!'

"He looked around, as if seeing the world for the first time. 'Where am I? What happened?' Then, remembering what the Lord had said about the work remaining to be done, he began testifying to the two unconverted doctors.

" 'Don Cesar,' one of them said, 'we have done nothing to bring you back. This has been a miracle of God.'

"And the dynamic change in his pastoral ministry is also a miracle! He has a new freedom and power, and an intensified love for souls."

Incredible Peace

Leslie Balogh, an attractive 28-year-old single parent, shared her experience with me while we were visiting her church in Arizona in 1989:

"I came back from death after I was in a car wreck ten years ago. My girlfriend and I, then only eighteen, were driving around a dangerous curve where several teenagers had been killed only the week before. When she lost control and the car overturned, I hit my head and knees and was thrown from the right seat of the car to the left where I was pinned underneath the steering wheel. They thought my back or my neck was broken. I heard one paramedic say to the other, 'She's dead; go get a sheet.' My girlfriend, with a good-sized cut over her eye, was by this time

out of the car, watching horrified as the man went to the ambulance to get the sheet.

"As I was dying, I went through a brief but uncomfortable
time of darkness, and then kept moving forward in the light
feeling all was O.K. Arriving in heaven was like a surprise birth-
day party. I mean a real surprise! I was greeted by three people,
two women and a man. Memory of the accident had been completely taken from my mind. The women spoke to me and told
me about the accident but told me not to look back at the car. I
am normally a very curious person but there I was completely
obedient. We apparently have an attachment to our physical bodies and at first there is a little sadness as we are parted from them.
My new friends tried to encourage me by showing me the good
things I had done on earth—the times I had witnessed for the
Lord.

"Communication there is the best possible. The first minute or
so when I arrived I was speaking to them in English, and then I
just transferred over to the language they were speaking, which
was not known to me. I caught on as we went along—receiving
this language of higher understanding as a gift. On earth I always
have to check to see if people are understanding me, but now in
this new language I knew exactly what they meant and they knew
exactly what I meant. Three paragraphs of words spoken here
might be about three words there.

"They asked me how I loved God. But they didn't want me to
answer in words. *The answer was my life and how I had lived it.*
They showed me my life, it was so vivid—like on a great VCR.
I said, 'If I had known this I'd have done so much more!' I felt
the gift I had for God was like the size box a ring comes in, while
others' gifts would be about the size box a refrigerator comes in.
They talked to me about my life, exhorting me; eventually the
man looked seriously at the women, as though to say, 'She can't
stay at this time, sisters.' Then they quickly explained to me that

I wouldn't remember all they said when I first returned to earth, but would recall much of it over the years. This has been true, and I have remembered things about it while reading Scripture or at other special times.

"When I came back from death, or near death, the contrast from heaven to earth was so amazing. Here at the accident were people screaming, stepping on glass, the grating sounds of metal as they tried to get me out of the smashed car. In heaven there was incredible peace and absolutely no stress. There I felt such love and compassion that I could have had love for anyone, even the most despicable person imaginable! The women had explained to me about the evil forces at work behind the scenes causing bad people to be as they are. I felt sorry for such people and I loved just everyone!

"When I awoke in the hospital, I told the nurse attending me what had happened. Her reaction was cynical and she strongly advised me to tell no one else or they would think I was crazy! This left me feeling a bit weird, lying there wondering if the awesome things I had experienced were true or not. Because of these wonders I had walked through and then, on the other hand, the conflicting attitude of the nurse, I was afraid to go to sleep, in case I might forget my experience of heaven. My mind was busy trying to sort things out, so during my wakefulness I prayed that God would somehow in the next week confirm to me what had really happened to me.

"At two o'clock in the morning the paramedic who helped me at the scene of the accident looked in my door. Surprised to find me awake, he came into the room and told me he had been compelled to drive back to the hospital to check on me. He sat down on the edge of the bed and said, 'I've been an atheist for thirty-two years of my life. I don't want to scare you—you're a young girl but—oh, forget it.' And then he just shook his head.

"Then he looked at me and asked, 'Do you believe in Jesus Christ?' I replied, 'Yes, I do.' His eyes brimmed with tears as he said, 'He saved your life tonight!'

"I began to cry and said, 'Yes, I know!'

"He went on, 'Everyone around the accident sensed something. And I'm going to go home tonight and stay on my knees until the sun rises, thanking Jesus that I knew it was Him!' "

Says Leslie, "This was God's immediate answer to me and the confirmation I needed. After the paramedic visited with me, I had such peace and fell asleep in a minute's time. I had been afraid to tell him about my visit to heaven, however, and it was a long time before I ventured again to share my story with anyone. Whenever I have shared it, it has given people hope, which, of course, gives me great joy. My little son, Joseph, can tell my story as well as I can!

"What a great night it was when my life was saved, and my paramedic's life was saved, too! In a few hours of time he changed from an atheist to a person who had a deeper relationship with Jesus Christ than I had at that time. I'm glad to say my commitment to Christ has continued to deepen since then."

A Place Prepared

These are only a few examples. There are more that I could share and more that others could share. It has been estimated that at least sixteen million people in recent times have had near-death experiences.[6] For those who want to believe, there is plenty of evidence that heaven is real. But many are so worried about being "taken in that they cannot be taken out" of their prison of doubt.[7] Some people abruptly dismiss all these pictorial concepts and claim that heaven is a state of being, but not a place. Scripture lets us know, however, that it is *both* a place and a state of being, and that it begins now. Some very assuring words of Jesus are: "I am going away to prepare a place for you. And when (if) I go and make ready a place for you, I will come back again and will take you to Myself, that where I am you may be also" (John 14:2–3, AMPLIFIED).

The time to make a decision is in this life, even if it's in the last microseconds of it. Jesus said, "I am the way and the truth and the life. No one comes to the Father except through me" (John 14:6, NIV). The clearest biblical example came while Jesus was dying on the cross, flanked on either side by thieves. One thief cursed Him. The other one begged that Jesus would remember him when He came into His Kingdom. To this man Jesus promised, "Today you will be with Me in Paradise" (Luke 23:43).

It's hard to understand how some people can see God, and yet not want Him, but this biblical example is very clear on this point. Again C. S. Lewis shows this truth vividly in *The Great Divorce*. He describes how some souls can be right at the door of heaven and find reasons not to go in.[8]

Where Is Heaven Located?

As wonderful as it is to know we have a heavenly home awaiting us—and glorious it is from all we've heard[9]—for now it's even more important to know that heaven has come to dwell in us. Jesus said, "The kingdom of God is within you," and, "The kingdom of heaven is at hand" (Luke 17:21; Matthew 10:7). Paul said that this truth, which has been revealed to the Church, is the greatest mystery of all the ages and of all generations, that is, "Christ in you, the hope of glory" (Colossians 1:27). The most important thing about heaven's location is that it is within you now, if you have received Jesus as your Savior.

A little bit of God's City is inside you. God has given you a taste of heaven as earnest money to assure you of the full value of your inheritance. Are you enjoying heaven within you right now? Drinking from the pure fountain, the refreshing rivers of living water that Jesus gave when you were spiritually reborn (John 7:38)? Feasting on delicious fruit of the Spirit from the inner Tree of Life—love, joy, peace (Galatians 5:22–23)?

You may not be able to explain to another person the physical location of heaven, but you can know and experience the deposit of heaven that is dwelling in your spirit, and at times flooding out through your soul and body. And you can help others on this earth receive this taste of heaven *now,* so that they will be assured of heaven *later.* I think it was Catherine of Siena who said, ''God gives us a little bit of heaven, to go to heaven in!''

Prayer

"In heaven . . ."

Dear Father, thank You that in Your Kingdom are many mansions and that Your Son is preparing one for me. What a glorious treasure and hope it is to know that I have the fullness of heaven to look forward to!

I'm eternally grateful, too, that heaven has come into my spirit right here and now as a down payment for that which is to come. I can never thank You enough for this gift! I breathe the breath of heaven, and touch Your hand, dear God; I'm walking in Your glory while still here on earth.

Show me how to allow heaven to flow through my life more effectively. Help me to be a good witness for You.

Pause and reflect

4
Holy Is Your Name

What do the words *holy, whole* and *health* all have in common?

If you go back into Middle and Old English language roots you will see that *holy* (*halig*), *whole* (*hal*) and *health* (*haelth*) have all descended from a common prototype.[1] This is also true of the same words in old high German.

Holy simply stated is "set apart to the service of God." *Whole* is "free of wound or injury, or recovered from a wound or injury." *Health* is "the condition of being sound in body, mind, or spirit."[2]

If you are dedicated to God and relating closely to Him, you will become *holy, whole* and *healthy*. These three attributes go together. This book could just as well have been called *Inner Holiness through the Lord's Prayer* or *Inner Health through the Lord's Prayer*. God is not only *holy*, but He is *whole* and *healthy*! The *holier* you are the more *whole* you'll be, and the more *whole* you are the *holier* you'll be. And the more *whole* you are the more likely you are to enjoy good *health*.

Wrote Merrill C. Tenny: "What became increasingly evident in the Old Testament is overwhelmingly explicit in the New Testament: that holiness means the pure, loving nature of God, separate from evil . . . and that it is to characterize human beings who have entered into personal relations with God."[3]

A "pure, loving nature separate from evil." How can you learn to live this way? How do you learn to talk this way? One answer is to use this prayer Jesus gave us frequently, preferably daily, and live it. Practice doing what Jesus tells you to do. Read through the Gospel records and the first chapter of Acts to see that His early followers considered it vitally important to put what He commanded into practice. Ask the Holy Spirit to show you how to do this. Live in that "first love" relationship with God and don't let yourself get stale or "Gospel-hardened."

Be childlike when you pray and when you think about the mystery of God. It makes no difference how old you are chronologically, because the Ancient of Days sees you as His child whether you are one or one hundred! Live in love and in the power of the Holy Spirit. Guard the anointing God gives you, as you would guard a treasure of precious stones.

Some people have tried to make holiness negative rather than positive. Behaving "holier than thou" can separate Christian from Christian. "To seek holiness apart from the other qualities of a Christlike life is to wander from the way of holiness itself," says the *Zondervan Dictionary*.[4] I believe that holiness—wholeness—should make you free to love, laugh, give, receive, stand for the right, be who you really are, get up wiser and stronger if you fall, affirm others, mend the broken, heal the world. This is what I hope for you as you pray the holy and healing prayer that our Lord gave us.

Honor His Name

If you put down members of your family, you're putting yourself down along with them. This is true also with your heavenly family—your Father in heaven, your Elder Brother, Jesus, and your Helper, the Holy Spirit. God's name is holy and to be honored. We're not to use it carelessly or drag it down with profanity.

I was fortunate that my parents, brothers and sister did not use profanity in our home while I was growing up. As a result I rarely did so myself even before I began my walk in the Spirit. This doesn't mean we were perfect, but happily this vice wasn't one I had to cope with. And now as an adult I can choose not to be around it.

Take movies, for instance. There are always a few good movies showing, but so many, even if the subject matter itself is worthwhile, are peppered with unnecessary profanity. Dennis and I have a number of times "voted with our feet" and walked out of a movie theater. Why should we take garbage into the temples of the Holy Spirit?

While on the subject of movies, I'd like to point out that what you choose to do can affect others as well, particularly your children. Now I don't think children should just be told "all movies are bad." They need to know how to choose the right ones themselves so the choice comes from *their* consciences, not just from *yours*. They are human beings, not machines, and they need to be taught to use their minds and grow in their capacity to choose.

But if you sit at home and watch a movie that is sexually explicit or profane, that causes your children to say to themselves, "My parent(s) approves of this, so it must be O.K. for me, too." Indiscriminate TV watching is dangerous if you want to live a life that honors God's name. What you allow to be viewed in your home, or away from it, for that matter, has your signature on it. Stop and think whether you would behave in front of your children as some of the characters on TV do.

Monitoring sounds and images is vitally important because the subconscious mind is deeply affected by what you hear and see. It does not discriminate. (A VCR is a big help here with selective TV watching.) You need to protect this part of your soul and not let negative things be put into it. That old saying is true, "What gets your mind gets you." Don't let yourself be controlled by any spirit other than the Holy Spirit.

It isn't good to be too rigid while trying to make decisions about things like TV or movie watching, but on the other hand, being too permissive isn't good either. Jesus can bring the balance when you make your decisions looking through His eyes.

Don't Misuse the Name of God

Why is Jesus' name, and God's name in general, so misused and abused? I once asked this question of a class I was leading and here are some of the answers:

"I think people swear and use profanity because they are frustrated, angry or dissatisfied. It's just the opposite of the peace and healing the Holy Spirit offers us."

"I think it's probably an attack of the enemy, trying to distort and malign our relationship with Jesus."

"I've noticed this in my work with men in construction. A lot of times I listen to them talking upstairs in the lunchroom. Most of the time they use profanity, and it strikes me that they think it makes them sound more manly or tougher to the men they're talking to. They're deceived into thinking they're brave, and so tough that they even dare to defy God by abusing His name."

"I think that a lot of times people don't know how to express themselves, or even to use the English language properly. They learned these profane words in grade school and junior high school and got into the habit of using them. They don't even think what they're doing."

"Since Jesus is so wonderful, and so many people love Him, it seems that the most daring thing they can do is say something really bad about Him. It makes them feel more powerful than God if they can put *God* down."

"If a person feels inadequate, he or she will tend to criticize others, and profanity is really criticizing God."

I think all these answers are helpful. You probably wouldn't like it if someone used your name as an expletive when he was angry or things were going wrong. I know I wouldn't like it if someone said, "Oh, Rita Bennett!" when he hit his finger, bumped his head or tripped! I'm sure God doesn't like it either when we associate His name with something bad that has happened. If you were brought up to do this, or if you hear a lot of it where you work, you may bring it home and use it in front of your family or friends. If you do, you need to ask them to forgive you, and, of course, ask God to forgive you, too.

Perhaps the Hebrews went too far in the other direction. Points out Merrill Tenny: "The Jews took seriously the third commandment 'Thou shalt not take the name of Jehovah thy God in vain . . .' (Exod. 20:7) and so, to keep from speaking the holy name carelessly, around 300 B.C. they decided not to pronounce it at all; but whenever in reading they came to it they spoke the [Hebrew] word *Adhonai* which means 'Lord.' "[5]

Because it was so rarely spoken, and because ancient Hebrew did not show the vowel sounds, in time they forgot how to pronounce the name of God at all. So all they had were the four consonants *jod, he, vau, he*.[6] (These letters JHVH, or YHWH are sometimes called the Tetragrammaton.[7]) Translators guessed at the pronunciation by adding to these consonants the vowels of *Adhonai,* thus making the name *Jehovah.* There is strong scholarly evidence that the holy name was pronounced "Yahweh." This form has been revived by modern scholars and is used quite generally today, but it is still only an educated guess at how the name was actually spoken.

The name seems to mean something like "I am He that is" or "He brings into existence all that is."

Thank goodness we don't have to know exactly how to say God's name and what vowel structure to use in order to speak to Him—whether to call Him Yahweh, Jehovah or Adhonai! Better still, we have the name of Jesus, which is the human name of God, and He tells us to pray in His name to the Father.

Descriptive Attributes of God

There are ten combinations of the name Jehovah, or Yahweh, in the Old Testament that describe what He is like:[8]

Jehovah-Shammah, Jehovah-Ropheka, Jehovah-Shalom, Jehovah-Tsidkenu, Jehovah-Meqaddeshkem, Jehovah-Roi, Jehovah-Tsabaoth, Jehovah-Nissi, Jehovah-Jireh, Jehovah-Elyon

In English these could be:

God is omnipresent, God is our Healer, God is our Peace, God is our Righteousness, God is our Sanctifier, God is our Shepherd, God is Lord of the armies of heaven, God is our Banner, God is our Provider, God is most high.

We'll look at each one of these titles in more detail. The well-loved Psalm 91 says, "Because he [God's child] has set his love upon Me, therefore I will deliver him; I will set him on high, because he has known My name" (verse 14). I certainly don't believe this means we must be able to quote these ten Hebrew proper names of God and their meanings in order to be delivered, but I do think that unless we have a broader picture of God and what He wants to do for us, we may *not* be delivered *simply because we don't know that it is our right to ask*. Reviewing these titles for Jehovah, or Yahweh, and their meanings, as we pray the Lord's Prayer will help keep before us a fuller picture of God and we will surely be delivered, just as the Scripture promises.

Jehovah-Shammah

God is omnipresent, here in all places and times. He is outside of the limitations of time and space. I list this attribute first because I believe *God's omnipresence is one of the master keys to inner wholeness*. (God's unconditional love is another, which we looked at in chapter 2.) When you see and enter into the truth that God's loving presence is with you in every moment of your life, from your conception to the present, and will be with you in every moment and place in the future, it can heal the way you feel about yourself and others, too.

Psalm 139:1–18 is one of the greatest passages on the ever-present God. It's a good one to memorize.

It says He was with you from the very beginning of your existence: "For You have formed my inward parts; You have covered me in my mother's womb" (verse 13), and it says there is no place you can go where He will not already be (verses 7–12).

Some of my other favorite Scriptures about God's omnipresence are:

"As the mountains are round about Jerusalem, so the Lord is round about His people from this time forth and for ever" (Psalm 125:2, AMPLIFIED).

" 'Can anyone hide himself in secret places, so I shall not see him?' says the Lord; 'do I not fill heaven and earth?' says the Lord" (Jeremiah 23:24).

"I am with you always" (Matthew 28:20).

"For in him we live, and move, and have our being" (Acts 17:28, KJV).

Søren Kierkegaard, Danish theologian, said, "Life must be lived forwards, but it can only be understood backwards."[9] I've found this true in my own life and have seen its truth numerous times with others. Each of us would find it beneficial to take a walk with God all the way through our lives, allowing Him to heal our memories and emotions as we go.

Jehovah-Ropheka

God is our Healer. Because we live in a fallen world, each of us has needed, needs presently or will need some degree of physical or psychological healing. Since we all need it, it is a good idea to appropriate as much as we can when we are praying. It's important to understand this gift of God so you will know how to receive it when you need it.

The Bible is full of promises for healing in body, soul and spirit. Exodus 15:26 gives four requirements to receive healing:

> (1) "If you will diligently hearken to the voice of the Lord your God, (2) and will do what is right in His sight, (3) and will listen to and obey His commandments (4) and keep all His statutes, I will put none of the diseases upon you which I brought upon the Egyptians; for I am the Lord Who heals you."
>
> AMPLIFIED

Make a trip through the first fifteen chapters of the Gospel according to Matthew and you will be amazed at how much time Jesus spent in healing people. Matthew 14:35–36 says they "brought to Him all who were sick, and begged Him that they might only touch the hem of His garment. And as many as touched it were made perfectly well."

Then there is the well-known prophecy in Isaiah 53:5 that says, "By His stripes we are healed" (see also 1 Peter 2:24). Psalm 103:3–5 says that God forgives all our sins, heals all our diseases, saves our lives from destruction, crowns us with lovingkindness and tender mercy, satisfies our mouths with good things, and renews our youth like the eagle's! There is no doubt but that the Father, Son and Holy Spirit are in the healing business!

Jehovah-Shalom

God is our Peace. God has placed an incredible heavenly peace within your reborn spirit. You need to enter into that peace, that *shalom*, so that it will permeate your thoughts, day by day. In these times of stressful living we need peace. This is not the peace of inactivity—lying around doing nothing (though there may be a time for that, too)—but it's an active peace that is with you even in your times of hardest work.

This title of God is used in the Authorized Version when Gideon was afraid he would die because he had seen an angel of the Lord face to face. "And the Lord said unto him, Peace be unto thee; fear not: thou shalt not die. Then Gideon built an altar there unto the Lord, and called it Jehovah-shalom" (Judges 6:23–24, KJV).

Jehovah-Tsidkenu

God is our Righteousness. The word translated "righteousness" in Hebrew really means "rightness"—not just moral rightness, but doing things in the right way. God is right in everything He does. We might say He is completely O.K.! You can enter into His presence, healing and peace by accepting His rightness.

You do not have any "O.K.ness" of your own. Your own good deeds may be commendable, but they cannot put you into right standing with God, or give you the right to make demands of Him. It's because of His grace (graciousness), His undeserved favor, His "love in action" provided through His Son that you come, as a child comes to a loving father.

Jehovah-Meqaddeshkem (abbreviated *m'qaddesh*)

God is our Sanctifier. Your spirit, the place where God lives in you, is holy because the Holy Spirit is there. But your soul—intellect, will, emotions, subconscious—is in the process of being made holy (whole, healthy, sanctified). That means, says Zondervan's *Bible Dictionary*, "the progressive conformation . . . into the image of Christ."[10] This is a gift of God, too, but you must receive it daily by looking to Him for strength and guidance in your life, which you have put into His hands. As you do this He will also strengthen you in your moral choices.

Holiness is provided for you in two ways: first, through the redemptive work of Christ, and second, through the indwelling and overflowing of the Holy Spirit in you. You try to give yourself to God (consecration), but He's the One who makes you whole, holy (sanctification). I like the verse in Philippians that says, "It is God who works in you both to will and to do for His good pleasure" (2:13). As you appropriate this, you are simply working *out* in your life what He worked *into* you when you were born again of the Holy Spirit.

Jehovah-Roi

God is our good Shepherd. Next to the Lord's Prayer, the Twenty-third Psalm is probably one of the best known and loved passages in the Bible. It may have been one of the first Scriptures you memorized. When I was writing an article on Psalm 23 for our teaching letter, *The Morning Watch*,[11] I noticed that the psalmist put his thoughts in a special order. He begins, "He restores my soul," and then follows with, "He leads me in the paths of righteousness." The longer I live the more I realize this is the order in which it must go.

You can't find the right path by your own efforts. You can't make yourself righteous, or sanctified, by your own efforts. The best way to walk on the right path is to seek to have your soul restored through prayer. The apostle James says, "Confess your faults one to another, and pray one for another, that ye may be healed" (James 5:16, KJV; this Scripture is discussed in some detail in *Emotionally Free*[12]). These faults are often defects in your soul that have been caused by things people have done against you. The Good Shepherd is faithful, and He will lead you to wholeness.

Jehovah-Tsabaoth

God is the Lord of the armies of heaven. This title of God is used 281 times in the Bible.

It was a great relief to me to discover I didn't have to fight my own battles, but that God and all the armies of heaven would fight for me. I was greatly helped by this Scripture: "Be not afraid or dismayed at this great multitude; for the battle is not yours but God's. . . . You shall not need to fight in this battle; take your position, stand still, and see the deliverance of the Lord" (2 Chronicles 20:15, 17, AMPLIFIED; be sure to read the entire chapter, perhaps in the KJV or NIV).

These verses refer to the time King Jehoshaphat and the Israelite army were told by the prophet Jahaziel to march to the place of battle but that they would not have to fight, as God would take care of the situation. The king consulted with the people and was led to put "singers unto the Lord, . . . that should praise the beauty of holiness, as they went out before the army" (verse 21, KJV). Praise is powerful artillery: As they sang and praised God, He caused the Moabites and the Ammonites and the Mount Seirites to attack one another and wipe themselves out! The enemy alliance was completely defeated without Israel's having to lift a sword.

Almost everyone knows how the Lord delivered the Israelites from the Egyptians (Exodus 14:13–31; 15:1–21). Then there was the time Elisha was surrounded at night by the Syrian army. His servant was terrified, but Elisha said, "Fear not; for those with us are more than those with them" (2 Kings 6:16, AMPLIFIED). Elisha asked God to open the young man's eyes so he could see God's chariots of fire 'round about them. Elisha prayed to God (not to the angels in the chariots) that the enemies would be blinded and confused; thus he was able to capture all of them. Later, when in safety, he mercifully prayed the Syrians' eyesight would be restored (see verses 1–23). So God and His army were there to rescue His people, and He is here to meet your needs, too.

Jehovah-Nissi

God is our Banner. In Scripture the term *banner* (flag, standard, ensign) can be used as a sign of victory to show a battle has been won; it can also be a rallying point for God's people. God says to Israel and to the Church—the spiritual Israel: "You have set up a banner for those who fear and worshipfully revere You— to which they may flee from the bow—a standard displayed because of the truth" (Psalm 60:4, AMPLIFIED).

One of my favorite verses and one many Christians have used when they've been in spiritual battle is: "When the enemy shall come in like a flood, the Spirit of the Lord will lift up a standard against him and put him to flight—for He [God] will come like a rushing stream which the breath of the Lord drives" (Isaiah 59:19, AMPLIFIED).

But this title points out God Himself as the Banner or the Standard around which Israel is to gather, as is shown clearly in verses 20 and 21.[13] God—Father, Son and Holy Spirit—is our sign of victory and our rallying point.

Jehovah-Jireh

God is our Provider. God provided for our first need when He gave Himself in His Son, Jesus, to take away our sins, making a brand-new race of people reborn in Him; and He continues to be the Provider for all our needs. Good parents who bring a child into the world don't simply bring him to birth and then provide for him for only a few months, but they continue to take care of him and give him the very best they can. So the word *salvation* not only refers to our being saved from our sins, but also means we are healed, fed, nurtured—in short, "provided for" in every way.

In the Bible there are hundreds of promises offered to the people of God, but as with any gifts, to be enjoyed they must be received. Here are a few of the many verses to consider:

"This book of the law shall not depart out of your mouth, but you shall meditate on it day and night, that you may observe and do according to all that is written in it; for then you shall make your way prosperous, and then you shall deal wisely and have good success" (Joshua 1:8, AMPLIFIED).

"And he sought God in the days of Zechariah, who had understanding in the visions of God: and as long as he sought the Lord, God made him to prosper" (2 Chronicles 26:5, KJV).

"I have been young, and now am old; yet have I not seen the righteous forsaken, nor his seed begging bread" (Psalm 37:25, KJV).

"And my God shall supply all your needs according to His riches in glory in Christ Jesus" (Philippians 4:19, NASB).

You need to learn from Scripture how you can live so you can enter into God-given prosperity. It is logical that God wants you, a member of His family, to have all you need, and to have extra so you can share it with others. Yet be sure to seek the Lord who gives prosperity, not the prosperity itself.

There are times in God's service when we choose work that is not prosperous financially, but rather spiritually. I'm thinking of the apostle Paul who said he knew how to be in want and how to prosper (Philippians 4:12). The way Paul phrased it shows he had chosen these things by his own initiative, because he concluded, "I can do all things through Christ who empowers me" (literal Greek). He experienced both, but it was by his own choice.

Some Christians feel that prosperity is a sign of God's blessing. Others feel the less you own, the more spiritual you are, and thus the more blessed you will be. We should be careful, however, not to judge another's spirituality based on prosperity or a lack of it.

God does want to bless us in every way possible, yet still the greatest blessing is to be in fellowship with Him, and working with Him, even though that sometimes may lead us to put up with literal hunger and thirst for the sake of the Gospel. The spiritual table will always be spread for us.

Jehovah-Elyon

God is most high. From *Dake's Annotated Reference Bible:* *"El* signifies Strong. . . . It is the title that shows God to be the Mighty One, the First Cause of everything, the possessor of the heavens and earth. It is used 250 times and is connected with some of the attributes of God as Almighty. . . ."[14] Jehovah-Elyon is used further to describe God as everlasting, living, merciful, faithful, mighty. This title is used 36 times in the Psalms alone.[15]

I put this particular attribute last, or tenth, as it sums up the picture well to conclude with the greatness of God. Though God is omnipotent, according to Zondervan's *Bible Dictionary* once again, "to a certain extent, He has voluntarily limited Himself by the free will of His rational creatures. Although the word 'omnipotence' is not found in the Bible, the Scriptures clearly teach [it]."[16] When Jesus was discussing the difficulty the rich have entering into heaven, the disciples asked, "Who then can be saved?" Jesus answered, "With men this is impossible, but with God all things are possible" (Matthew 19:25, 26). When the angel visited the virgin Mary to tell her she was chosen to bring the Son of God into the world, he said to her, "For with God nothing will be impossible" (Luke 1:37). The psalmist said, "That men may know that You, whose name alone is the Lord, are the Most High over all the earth" (83:18). And again, "I will praise the Lord according to His righteousness, and will sing praise to the name of the Lord Most High" (7:17). Good advice for us all to follow!

Attributes of God in the Trinity

Did you notice that all these attributes sound as if they apply to Jesus, too? They do. Just as we can't divide the Trinity, we shouldn't apply these attributes to only one member of the triune Godhead—Father, Son or Holy Spirit. I'm emphasizing God the Father in this discussion because we don't often see Him in these nurturing kinds of roles.

You have come to know this wonderful Father personally, if you have let Jesus bring you to Him. You may not know how to say the name of God the way the ancient Hebrews did, but you know how to say His Son's name, and it is through Him you can know God and call Him, as Jesus did, "Abba, Father!"

What do *you* have in common with the words *holy, whole, health?* They speak of you because your spirit, which is joined to God, has these three qualities, and your soul and body are also in the process of becoming more like your Father, day by day.

Prayer

"Holy is Your name . . ."

Dear Father, I'm so glad that I know You in person through Your Son, Jesus, who comes to me by the power of the Holy Spirit. Help me treat You and Your name, as well as Your Son's name, and the Holy Spirit's name, with the full love and respect deserved. [*When appropriate add: Forgive me when I haven't done this.*]

You alone are fully holy and fully whole. Please fill my life more and more with this holiness, this wholesomeness.

I thank You, Father, for all the dimensions of Your name. Thinking about these attributes, one by one, enriches my relationship with You and my appreciation of You. You are a mighty and wonderful God!

Pause and reflect.

5
Your Kingdom Come

"The wolf also shall dwell with the lamb, and the leopard shall lie down with the kid; and the calf and the young lion and the fatling together; and a little child shall lead them" (Isaiah 11:6, KJV).

When we read these beautiful words, we often picture the artist's interpretation of them in "The Peaceable Kingdom," which shows a little child with an arm around an ox, and the lamb and the lion standing together without fear. The lion and the lamb is a familiar theme for greeting cards each year at Christmastime and refers to the reign of Christ on the earth after it has been restored (see Isaiah 11:1–10).

There will be no more killing, hate, greed, revenge, sickness, death—no more demonic activity. But that's still to come. What about *now*? Can we enter into some of these benefits now?

The apostle Paul thought so. He wrote, "The kingdom of God

is . . . righteousness and peace and joy in the Holy Spirit'' (Romans 14:17). And Jesus said, ''Seek first the kingdom of God and His righteousness'' (Matthew 6:33) and, ''Do not be afraid, little flock, for your Father has been pleased to give you the kingdom'' (Luke 12:32, NIV). All these surely refer to a Kingdom that can be enjoyed now.

Explains *The New Bible Dictionary,* ''The kingdom of heaven or kingdom of God[1] is the central theme of Jesus' preaching, according to the Synoptic Gospels.''[2] But what is this Kingdom of God? What are its hallmarks? Why did Jesus ask us to pray for it to come?

I once asked these questions of a class at a retreat and these were some of their answers:

''The Bible says that things were spoken into being at creation. As we speak God's words in the Lord's Prayer about the Kingdom, we, too, are helping bring it to pass. Also, we see from the history of the Hebrew children, from traditions they kept, that they repeated frequently the stories of God's interactions with them. We need to do the same so we'll always remember, because, funny as it is, we can forget. Repeating these words over and over again out loud helps us *not* forget.''

''Praying these words gives us hope that the Kingdom really is coming. Something great to look forward to!''

''The sense that I get out of the phrase *Thy Kingdom come* is that it's not only a prayer but also a declaration. It's not 'Well, maybe it'll come' or 'Possibly it'll come' or 'We hope it'll come'; it's 'Thy Kingdom come.' We're making a statement of faith, and it's far stronger than mere speculation.''

''It is saying the Kingdom is here. But we have the authority to refuse it. There's no sin, there's no disease, there's none of this stuff in His Kingdom that we're so accustomed to on earth, so maybe we shouldn't be accepting some of the negative happenings in our lives!''

These were all helpful off-the-cuff answers: a powerful confession, a reminder lest we forget, an expectation, a statement of faith, a revelation: His Kingdom is here—now!

Where and What Is the Kingdom?

God is King, and He has a Kingdom over which He rules. After you have invited the "King of kings," Jesus Christ, to live in you, His Kingdom has come inside you and He can rule through you. The Kingdom is wherever the King is. He said, "For indeed, the kingdom of God is within you" (Luke 17:21). He often said, "The Kingdom of heaven is at hand" or "nearby." In fact, the Gospels list 114 times Jesus mentioned the Kingdom. In a way, Jesus Himself is the Kingdom on earth and He also manifests it. From *The New Bible Dictionary* again: "The kingdom has come in Him and with Him; He is the *autobasileia*. . . . [It] is concentrated in Him in its present and future aspects alike."[3]

What is the Kingdom like and how will we recognize it? *The New Bible Dictionary* says, ". . . John the Baptist points to the coming One who is to follow him, whose forerunner he himself is. . . . In view of His coming the people must repent and submit to baptism for the washing away of sins, so as to escape the coming wrath and participate in the salvation of the kingdom and the baptism with the Holy Spirit which will be poured out when it comes (Mt. iii. 1–12)."[4] The Kingdom "appears palpably and visibly in the casting out of demons (cf. Lk. xi. 20) and generally in Jesus' miraculous power."[5] The supernatural gifts of the Spirit are proof of the coming of the Kingdom. John the Baptist sent his disciples to ask if Jesus was the Messiah, the One to bring in the Kingdom. Jesus' answer was, "Go and tell John the things which you hear and see: The blind receive their sight and the lame walk; the lepers are cleansed and the deaf hear; the dead are raised up and the poor have the gospel preached to them'' (Matthew 11:4–5). This then is the Kingdom in action.

What is the Gospel (Good News) of the Kingdom we are to proclaim? It's teaching people that the Kingdom of heaven is here and can be entered now, and helping them do so. Only by child-like faith can a person enter—actually see and experience—the Kingdom (John 3:3, 5). It's proclaiming the need to: repent, be converted and reborn of the Spirit (through Jesus' death and resurrection), be baptized, be empowered or baptized with the Holy Spirit, forgive, love, learn about authority in Christ (your keys of the Kingdom), cast out evil spirits, heal the sick in body and soul, receive angelic aid, learn the value of praising God, receive His gifts, receive Him in the Communion of the Lord's Supper. It's seeing to it that these and all other teachings of Jesus are proclaimed to all nations on the earth. He said, ''Go therefore and make disciples of all the nations . . . teaching them to observe all things that I have commanded you; and lo, I am with you always, even to the end of the age'' (Matthew 28:19–20).

Is It Necessary to Keep Praying for It?

God's Kingdom already is, or it could not come to earth, says *The Interpreter's Bible*.[6] But is it necessary to continue praying these words *Thy Kingdom come*, since God's Kingdom has already come in and through Jesus Christ and in His people? Yes and no. (This is always a safe answer!) No, in that you, as a believer, don't need to continue asking God to place His Kingdom in your spirit, which has become ''God's permanent dwelling place,'' but rather to thank Him that He's already come.

Yes, because by continuing to pray, ''Thy Kingdom come'' with *understanding* and *faith,* you are helping to bring His Kingdom of joy and freedom to pass in two other ways. First, even though His Kingdom has come in your spirit, your soul—which is composed of your intellect, will, emotions and subconscious—has many "rooms" and not all of them are fully opened to God. How do I know this? Because I, too, know there are areas in my soul that need God's further healing and sanctifying work, and this varies from time to time according to my circumstances. My friends and others I come in contact with tell me the same thing about themselves. So I believe you should pray these words with the invitation for God to become more fully in charge of your soul life, because if you aren't healed, you can become a negative example to those who look up to you. The psalmist David said it this way: "Search me, O God, and know my heart: try me, and know my thoughts" (Psalm 139:23, KJV).

Some of God's Kingdom was restored to earth when you received Jesus into your life, and more is being restored as you let Him work in and then through you. You can help the Kingdom be seen on earth right now by becoming a more whole person yourself, and passing that wholeness on to your family and others. Asking Him to set up His rule in your soul will affect everything around you from your own body, to your household, to everyone you come in contact with directly or by telephone, to letters and literature you write, to your talents and abilities. Whatever is under God's Lordship is part of the Kingdom of God; that includes your thoughts, your speech, your money, your clothes, your car, your entertainment, your work, your home. . . .

Second, you can use it as an intercessory prayer and a means of spiritual warfare, claiming others for God's Kingdom. "Thy Kingdom come" is a vital evangelistic prayer for us all to be using until Jesus returns. The ancient Jews believed that "he prays not at all, in whose prayers there is no mention of the kingdom of God."[7] This petition in the Lord's Prayer is one powerful way to help the Kingdom of God be brought to earth; in fact, God is *counting on your prayers* to help bring about the full harvest of His Kingdom.

Be careful, by the way, never to think this can be done in your own strength or else you may think it depends on you alone. Instead remember that it comes in and through Jesus Christ and the Holy Spirit, and you are a part of the process.

View the Kingdom in Three Dimensions

The Kingdom of God is three-dimensional: *The Kingdom has come, the Kingdom is coming* and *the Kingdom will come.* To understand it more fully you must view it from this threefold understanding of past, present and future.

His Kingdom has come and set up headquarters in your spirit. His Kingdom is coming more and more into your soul life, and through you and your prayers to reach the lost. His Kingdom is coming in its fullness when He will reign forever and ever.

If you have only one of these dimensions in mind, then you will miss God's full purpose. If you believe the Kingdom has fully come, then you will see no reason to keep on praying for it to come to earth, and will miss out on the great importance God places on this intercessory prayer for yourself and others. You must also believe the Kingdom is coming, and work to bring that to pass. Likewise, if you believe the Kingdom will come but has in no part arrived, you may think its benefits are not for today and sit back and do nothing—and receive nothing—waiting for it.

What a great assurance we have to learn from God Himself the words and manner in which He would have us pray. When a king receives a petition that he has guided a citizen to draw up, you can be sure that he has the fullest intention of granting the request. You are praying according to God's will and so all heaven is backing you up when you pray, "Thy Kingdom come."

Prayer

"Your Kingdom Come . . ."

Dear Father, thank You that the Kingdom of heaven has taken up its permanent dwelling place in me, in my spirit. Please bring into my soul all the wholeness I can possibly receive. I want to be a good representative of Yours through Your Son, Christ Jesus. I want to help bring Your Kingdom to others through prayer and through being a good witness.

May my eyes show Your Kingdom. May my words speak Your Kingdom. May my ears hear Your Kingdom. May my hands assist Your Kingdom. May my touch reveal Your Kingdom. May my responses to others bring Your Kingdom. Let there be a little patch of heaven everywhere I go.

Pause, reflect and praise.

6
Your Will Be Done

"There are only two kinds of people in the end: those who say to God, 'Thy will be done,' and those to whom God says, in the end, 'Thy will be done.' " (So George MacDonald is imagined saying in *The Great Divorce*.[1]) What an awful feeling to think God might finally have to say those words, *Your will be done!* When we look at it in those terms we think, *How can there be any question about it? Of course I want God's will to be done, and not mine!* But when we're in the midst of life's choices we are swayed in many different directions. Our perspective seems sometimes like the reflections in a hall of mirrors at a carnival fun house.

Human freedom causes unimaginable problems, yet even when you turn your life over to God, He doesn't take your free will away. He doesn't possess your will or want you to give it up; He wants you to allow Him to guide you and inspire you so that you want what He wants. As Psalm 40:8 expresses it, "I delight to do Your will, O my God." It is with this attitude Jesus tells us to pray, "Your will be done." It's absolutely vital if God's plan is to be carried out on the earth that you joyfully align your will with God's—not just initially, but daily, hourly.

Each time you yield your will to God you are saying to Him, "I love You." That blesses Him just as it blesses a parent to have his children do what he wants them to because they love and want to please him (or her). Jesus was constantly submitted to His Father, and this should be your goal, too. He said, "I do not seek My own will but the will of the Father who sent Me" (John 5:30; also see John 5:19 and Matthew 26:39), and this is repeated in many places throughout the Gospel of John. We need to learn how to do this, too.

Free Will: A Priceless Gift

When God created you He gave you the priceless gift of free will; it is part of the image of God in you. He could not take it away without totally changing your created nature. Without free will you would be a robot, not a human being. You could not choose to love God Himself unless you were free, and yet, with this gift, you could also choose to work against your Creator—to rebel against Him. When the first man and woman chose to go this way, it caused the fall of the human race and made necessary the most costly remedy of all time: the life of God's Son, given to release our wills from Satan's grasp.

Your will is free, but as you bring it into line with what God wants He can guide you and bring you His best. I sometimes picture my will as a swinging door between my soul and spirit. The question is, Which way is it going to swing? I, by my choice, can determine whether my decision will come from God, who dwells in my recreated spirit, or from my soul, which is still in the process of being healed.

"The will of God," says *Clarke's Commentary*, "is infinitely good, wise, and holy; to have it fulfilled in and among men, is to have infinite goodness, wisdom, and holiness diffused throughout the universe; and earth made the counterpart of heaven."[2] More people need to be convinced of this goodness of God. It's hard to yield your will to another unless you can trust that he wants the very best for you and that his wisdom is greater than yours.

Some Are Afraid to Pray It

Often when people give their lives to God they are afraid He will send them to the most forlorn location known on earth to do His work! The Kingdom of God is a realm of joy and peace. Why do we regard it as a threat to our joy and fulfillment? "Thy will be done" should be a prayer we pray confidently with complete trust in God's care for us. This is not to say that some won't be led to difficult and dangerous places, but if God sends them they will find complete fulfillment and total satisfaction in that work.

If you especially enjoy a particular kind of work, and seem well-equipped for it, why should not God want you to do it for Him? He is the One who equipped you and gave you the desire to do it.

Those who have been abused emotionally or physically, especially in childhood, are sometimes afraid to pray this part of the Lord's Prayer because they're not really sure God loves them or wants the best for them. A friend of mine said she used to be afraid to pray, "Thy will be done," for fear God would beat her over the head! Such opinions of God are based on a person's experience with parents or parent figures (chiefly with fathers, but mothers, too) or with other people who had authority over them, especially in childhood. They will need prayer for inner wholeness before they can deepen their commitment to God.

Another way people are programmed negatively is by being taught an extreme, unbalanced sovereignty-of-God position. If destructive things happen in their lives or to others, they hear, "God did this" or, "If God loved us He wouldn't have let this happen." This thinking ignores the effects of sin in the world. It also overlooks the fact that although God is the King, He is also perfect love: To relegate everything from hurricanes to premature deaths in children as God's will is destructive theology. It's no wonder so many people have avoided God, and stayed away from churches!

Crushed Will or Stubborn Will

People whose wills have been crushed react strongly to the idea of allowing God's will free reign in their lives. Christian teachers will sometimes speak as though God wants to "break" His followers. It is a poor word choice as it normally implies destructive action. God doesn't want to break our wills in the sense of destroying them, but in the sense in which we "break" a horse from a wild state to a workable and usable one.

Bek had a poor relationship with her mother who had spanked her so severely when she was ten years old that Bek felt her will had become lifeless, like a limp rag. Being molested in infancy, and again in childhood, set up her foundation of hurts. Just looking at Bek you could see the results of her crushed will: downcast eyes, slumped shoulders and passive manner. During a time of prayer in which she sought healing for her soul, she gave her will to Jesus, and the Master Potter took her limp will into His hands, renewed and remolded it, put His light into it and replaced it in her soul. This was a major key to her healing although it took many other prayers to complete it.[3]

Persons with stubborn and sometimes aggressive wills also react against the idea of turning their wills over to God. Such people often come from the school of hard knocks in more ways than one. Their difficult formative years caused them to develop this stubbornly strong will in order to survive. Yet what was necessary at one time now will be a hindrance to growth unless it's submitted to God. While being healed, such persons will need to pray more often to yield their wills than those who have not been so damaged by life.

If you feel your will is damaged, then you need to realize that your loving Father doesn't want to crush it further, but to strengthen it and heal it from being passive and weak. If your will is aggressively stubborn, on the other hand, you need to release it to Him to become more pliable. Some of your stubbornness may need to be softened and brought into submission before God is able fully to do His will through you.

If you need healing in either of these ways, or others, be sure to take some time with loving and knowledgeable friends to pray for it.

God Wants You to Be Happy

Salvation of the spirit means the joining of God's Spirit with your human spirit so that it is reborn and the two become as one (1 Corinthians 6:17). Then, says *Clarke's Commentary* "the salvation of the soul is the result of two wills conjoined: the will of God, and the will of man."[4] I like Adam Clarke's choice of the word *conjoin* because it means two separate and individual entities joined together in purpose; God doesn't lessen our identities when we yield to Him but makes us more fully ourselves. Our souls cannot be happy and fulfilled until our wills are submitted to and at one with God's will. St. Augustine said it this way: "Thou hast formed us for Thyself, and our hearts are restless till they find rest in Thee."[5]

Dennis and I wrote in *Trinity of Man:* "God wants us freely to pattern our wills after His, to let the Holy Spirit in us conform our will to His so we want the same thing He wants because His nature is in us."[6] Ultimately God wants us to want what He wants, and thoroughly enjoy doing it because it will bring us the most happiness.

Prayer

"Your will be done . . ."

Dear Lord, I pray for Your will to be done in me and around me. I yield my will to You today. *Will* through me. *Love* through me. *Think* through me. Please show me how to follow You, and when I don't catch Your cues, turn things to good regardless of my mistakes. I want my heart to be always toward You. [*When appropriate add: Heal my will so I can be more open to You and Your good plans for me.*]

I'm so glad to know that You want to make me happy and fulfilled. Help me trust You so much that I can say as Jesus did, "I do not seek My own will but the will of My Father. . . ." And as the psalmist said, "I delight to do Your will, O my God." Your will be done, Lord!

Pause and reflect.

7
On Earth As in Heaven

"On earth as in heaven" means to me that God wants His children well, because in heaven no one is sick, sad, in pain, fearful, angry or depressed. Not only is everyone experiencing the epitome of health, but joy, peace and love as well. Since God Himself told you to pray for the blessings of heaven to be on the earth, He obviously wants you to be healthy and happy. The apostle Luke puts Jesus' words this way: "As in heaven, so in earth" (Luke 11:2, KJV). To the same degree that God's will is being done in heaven, He desires it done in earth.

Jesus must have meant for us to pray for the ways, the atmosphere, the attitudes of heaven to come on earth. If it weren't possible, I'm sure He wouldn't have asked His Church to pray for it. Jesus told His disciples to say, "The kingdom of God has come near to you," as they healed the sick (Luke 10:9). He took it for granted that they would do what He did.

Suppose you visited a wealthy person's palatial home, which was furnished with the most elegant antiques, drapes, Oriental rugs, priceless paintings, chests of sterling silver, shelves of crystal and china with gorgeous patterns, Tiffany chandeliers, the most advanced appliances; and the owner were to say this to you: "Everything I have here in my home I am going to make available to you for your home. I'm calling my interior decorator right now and will ask her to duplicate everything I have. If you choose different colors and styles, that will be fine, of course. My desire is to make you totally happy by offering what has been done in my house to be done in your house. There's no charge to you, and no strings attached; I only want you to be completely happy, as I am."

Your answer would probably be, "Well, that sounds great, but I've never heard of such a thing being done! It's hard to believe."

But hasn't God the Father said something like this to you? "All I have is yours," He tells us. "I want you to have everything on earth that I have in heaven. I've made it available to you. All you have to do is love, believe in and follow Me, and by your childlike faith you will receive everything you need. It is My joy to give you the Kingdom; there are no strings attached. My only desire is for you to be completely happy as I am. Ask in My Son's name and you will receive it."

What will you answer? "That sounds great, but are You really sure it's for me? I find it hard to believe." Or will you say, "It sounds wonderful; I will dare to believe and with Your help I will overcome any unbelief."

A fountain of life and a fruitful tree of health and love are in heaven. God must want us to enter into these gifts now. They are part of the furnishings of heaven.

Doctors Cooperating with God

One of the main things that comes to mind when we think of heaven is that there is no pain or sickness there. And this, by the way, means that medical doctors and nurses on earth must be cooperating with God because they are trying to make people well—to help eliminate sickness from the earth. It surprises me when someone says, "It is the will of God that I'm sick," and then promptly goes to a doctor to get medicine to counteract the illness or disease. Doesn't this put the poor doctor in a very awkward position, since he seemingly would be opposing God's will by trying to bring health to the person?

Men and women in medicine have risked their lives to bring healing to others. A well-known example is that of army doctor James Carroll, who allowed himself to be bitten by an infected mosquito to prove that yellow fever was transmitted in this way. People like him are doing God's will and hazarding their own lives to do so. I appreciate, too, the doctors, especially in preventative medicine, who have helped so many, including me.

Human medicine can do a lot of marvelous things these days, although there are a lot of things it cannot do. God isn't going to desert you because you find you aren't able at the time to receive healing directly from Him. Both God and the doctor want you well and healthy! If, on the other hand, you can trust and receive "repairs" from the Manufacturer Himself, that is certainly the best way to go. Remember, if you are healed by the Lord directly, tell your doctor about it; he may be happy, too. And if you've been on medication, he will tell how and when you can safely stop using it.

My great-grandfather Peter William Reed, a Scotsman, was one of the early medical doctors in the U.S. When he was three or four years old, a boy threw sand in his face, which gave him ulcerated and running eyes. He became virtually blind, except for being able to see light and dark. His older brother, Sandy, walked with him to school each day and helped him with his studies all the way through high school. When he was around twenty, he and Sandy went to a sale on a farm in Michigan where a large medical book was auctioned off. Peter purchased the book for fifty cents, which was a good deal of money for a young man to spend in those days. He was interested in medicine, perhaps in part because he had been to a number of doctors—who unfortunately could do nothing for him. That day at the auction he had a sudden thought: *This book might give me information to help me regain my sight.*

Later at home his faithful brother, Sandy, read through the prescriptions on the care of eyes. They tried more than twenty of them, and finally one prescription began to clear up Peter's sight! A kind of scum came off his eyes and he was able to see again. He then went on with his studies to become a doctor and to help others. That's a story of guidance in a natural way, and certainly one showing the great value of persistence. My great-grandfather Reed didn't know about healing gifts available through prayer, but God found an avenue of healing for him in a way he could receive it.

My older brother, Dr. William Standish Reed, in the course of his long and successful surgical career, has many times laid hands on the sick and seen them recover without the aid of his medical skills.[1] He has also helped heal many people through those skills he spent years in medical school acquiring. I know quite a number of Christian doctors, and nurses, too, who pray for their patients in the office or the operating room, and sometimes striking healings take place.

Expect Healing

We have died out of Adam's fallen race and have been born into a new race of people, through Jesus Christ. As we learn to walk in this new dimension, miracles happen. The more we strengthen our belief in miracles and live in expectation of them, the more they can happen; if healing were not possible, God would not have told us to pray, "Thy Kingdom come on earth, as it is in heaven." After all, Psalm 103:3 says that the Lord God "forgives all my sins, and heals all my diseases" (GNB). The Gospels tell us over and over again that Jesus healed "all that were sick" (Matthew 8:16; 9:35; et. al.). The first disciples had the same results. Jesus gave them power, even while He was still on earth with them, to heal "all kinds of sickness and all kinds of disease" (Matthew 10:1), and He made it clear that He intended His followers to continue to do so.

What if you ask for healing but it hasn't happened yet? When you don't accept your illness or the diagnosis of your disease as the final word, professional people may say you are "in denial." But if you've prayed and know that God has touched you, I don't think it's "denial" to make a positive confession such as, "Yes, there is a physical problem, but I believe Jesus is healing me and I'm expecting to see the manifestation of it." If you are still waiting to receive your healing, keep praying. Since Jesus Christ never said no to anyone who asked for healing, you have every reason to believe Him for it. And remember how God led my great-grandfather to healing in a natural way with what I believe was supernatural guidance. A doctor's diagnosis may help you by showing you where and how you are being attacked and God may use a doctor's expertise to heal you, but also realize God is not limited by man's diagnostic wisdom or fatal predictions, but can reverse and cure the most hopeless problems.

It's highly important, too, that we cooperate with God in taking proper care of our physical bodies, that we avoid stress as much as we can, and pay attention to proper nutrition and exercise.

Some Healing Examples

When we teach healing we have people pray for each other, and many are healed. Mostly small problems like headaches or back pain—but more serious things may be healed, too: heart disease, cancer, stomach ulcers, goiter, asthma, etc. Small healings, we find, build faith for big ones.

Recently Dennis and I each had small but wonderful healings. While cooking, I spilled some boiling oil on my little finger. I stuck it quickly under cold water and Dennis prayed for it. When I had burned myself before, cold water helped but didn't cure the effects of the burn. This time, within minutes after prayer, the pain stopped and I watched the redness fade away until there was no sign at all that the finger had been burned.

That same weekend Dennis started coming down with the usual symptoms of the flu. I prayed for him, and by the next morning he was totally normal.

It is significant that we had been reading faith-building books together each evening for some months, which increased our openness to receive from God.

Then there are the "big ones." Some years ago a friend fractured ten bones in an accident, including his pelvis and a depressed skull. He was not expected to live, but the Lord healed him and he was dismissed from the hospital in three days. The doctor offered to show anyone the before-and-after X-rays!

A man in Victoria, British Columbia, was healed of Paget's disease. He had been told it was incurable and that he would need a hip replacement. After being prayed with he said, "It was as though electricity went through my body." He was also healed of arthritis. He reported to us later that he was swimming daily and doing springboard diving!

A twelve-year-old was healed of a stomach ulcer. His parents wrote to us saying this was confirmed by X-ray, and that the doctor was pleased to hear about the power of prayer.

These are just a few examples of God's will being done on earth. He does heal supernaturally today, and He wants to heal *you*!

Receive and Pass On Healing

Some may wonder, If we keep on getting healed, when will we die? Unfortunately this is rarely the big problem we have to contend with! We know we won't always live on this earth in its present state, or in our present state. One thing we are promised and look forward to is having resurrected bodies, like Jesus' body. But I like the idea I gleaned from a teacher at an Order of Saint Luke's healing seminar many years ago: When we die we don't have to be like green apples that fall from the tree prematurely because worms have ravaged them, but we can be like rosy, fully matured apples that fall from the tree in the fullness of time from the weight of their ripeness.

The more we study our human bodies, which are so "fearfully and wonderfully made," the more amazed we are with the backup systems that are built in and the way our bodies work to heal themselves. Wherever we look at God's creation, we see His healing handiwork.

I believe God is always trying to speak to us, to help us and to heal us. He wants us to be in good health for our joy, and so we can be doing the work of bringing others the Good News of the Kingdom. One of the purposes of this book is to make you more open to God so He can speak clearly to you, and so that you can receive the healing gifts He has for you whether they are for physical or psychological needs.

In the original English Prayer Book of 1549, the words from the Lord's Prayer are translated, "Thy will be done *in* earth as it is in heaven," and this is the way it appears in the Authorized Version of the Bible. The Greek text is clear enough, "Thy will be done [*epi tes ges*] upon the earth," and the early English translators were no doubt simply following the idiom of their day when they said "in earth." But I like that way of saying it, too, because the work must begin *in* us, and then go out to the world *through* us.

One of Jesus' first commands to His followers was, "Heal the sick. . . . Freely you have received, freely give" (Matthew 10:8). The disputed ending of Mark (verses 9–20) says that one of the signs to follow believers is "they will lay hands on the sick, and they will recover" (16:18). Whether this was in the earliest manuscripts or not, it certainly agrees with the experience of believers in the New Testament, and on down to the present. So as you receive God's healing gifts—meant for us on earth as in heaven—don't forget to pass them on.

Prayer

"On earth as it is in heaven . . ."

Dear Father, I thank You that Your Kingdom is being established on this planet earth as it is being established in me. Please change anything in me that works against Your plan for Kingdom living. Thank You for the glorious fact that You, triune God—Father, Son and Holy Spirit—are living in Your children's spirits and, when allowed, overflow into our souls (emotions, memories, intellects, wills, personalities), into our bodies and out to others. Use us to bring Your healing Kingdom to others.

Help me to tap into Your healing power so it can flow into me today to meet my physical and emotional needs, those known and those unknown to me. May I enter into the many benefits of heaven that You've provided for those who love You. I claim Your will to be done in me and my household this day, even as it is in heaven.

Pause, reflect and praise.

94

8
Give Us Today
Our Daily Bread

Have you ever flown over a large city at night and looked out the plane's window at those hundreds of thousands of twinkling lights shining from homes, stores, streetlights and wondered, "How can there be enough food for all those people, eating three meals a day, three hundred and sixty-five days a year, year after year?" I know I have done this and felt awed by it. Then multiply the lights of that one community by the thousands of communities in hundreds of nations on earth and it is even more mind-boggling.

What does "daily bread" bring to your thoughts? Is it white bread or whole grain bread, French bread or German bread, sourdough bread or Ezekiel seven-grain bread, sprouted wheat or rye bread, sunflower seed bread, oatmeal bread, soy bread, cornbread, pocket bread? Is it with or without yeast, oil, salt, preservatives, sugar, eggs or even flour? You name it! There is some kind of bread you can eat—that is, unless you are on a weight-loss program that for a time eliminates all bread!

The Gospel according to Matthew records that Jesus on two occasions miraculously fed thousands of people with fish and a few loaves of bread. At both times the crowd—one of five thousand men, one of four thousand men, besides women and children—had been so caught up with Jesus' words, the power of His presence and His healings and other mighty acts that they forgot all about eating. (I've heard a lot of excellent ministers, evangelists and teachers in the last thirty years but I've never heard one who could keep a crowd enthralled for three days without their stopping to eat!) Jesus didn't want to send the people home without food because they might collapse from hunger as they went (Matthew 15:32), so He fed them supernaturally. Jesus apparently enjoyed giving "bread and fish dinners" because He did it three times that I know of. The third time was after His resurrection, when He fed the disciples on the lake shore (John 21:1–14).

The kind of bread made at that time was whole grain because they didn't have the equipment to refine it—that is, strip vitamins, minerals and fiber from the flour. Complex carbohydrates and protein, we might call a meal of bread and fish today. Pretty healthy fare, and in company with the Bread of Life Himself!

When I get to this part of the Lord's Prayer, I pray as a wife and homemaker that God will show me what to feed my husband and myself that day, or the next day. It takes quite a bit of study, ingenuity and creativity to come up with healthful daily meals. What you put into your body is very important and perhaps I'm trying to make up for the years that I paid little attention to what was good for me. I guess at one time I thought the only acceptable sin involved food! I'm not perfect in this area but I've been working at it for the past 22 years. It takes time and effort but it's worth it if you want to live life to its fullest. I believe I should take care of my body at least as well as I do my home and car.

Bread for Today

There are more than thirty different possible meanings for the words used in the original Greek manuscripts of Matthew and Luke that are translated "daily bread." I was impressed with the selection of categories for this word in *The Greek-English Lexicon*. First is bread "for the current day, for today"; second is bread "for the following day"; and third is bread "for the future."[1] Bread for the present, for tomorrow and for the future—that's *total* care from our triune God!

We are to pray, "Give us *today*." God tells us to ask Him for our needs to be met daily so we will keep in mind that He is the source of our supply. Remember, one of the descriptive names of God in the Old Testament is *Jehovah-Jireh*, which means "God will see to it," that is, He will provide. Jesus knew only too well that we need to be reminded to depend on His Father. He said to consider the lilies, and to know that God is aware even when a sparrow falls (Matthew 6:25–34; 10:29). Bread is a free gift of God's grace. God gives it to us because He loves us, not because we always deserve it.

The Interpreter's Bible says, "The saint even in his prayers is still dependent on bread. So this prayer is a confession of need. No man has 'independent means': he cannot eat dollar bills for breakfast."[2]

God is concerned about our individual needs, but notice it's not just give *me* this day *my* daily bread, but *us our* daily bread. God doesn't want us to be self-centered. In our prayers and also in our daily lives, He wants us to reach out to others. We need not only to pray for the poor, but also to feed them.

Bread for Tomorrow and the Future

Since "daily bread" also means bread for tomorrow and thereafter, it means you shouldn't be worried and anxious about your food. The meaning is, "You will have your essential day-to-day needs met." You may not always be given a banquet (a constant banquet wouldn't be good for you anyway!), but you can claim and have all you need daily if and as you live in right relationship with God and man (Psalm 37:25).

The apostle Paul writes to the Philippians: "My God shall supply all your need according to His riches in glory by Christ Jesus" (4:19). Since God created everything in the first place, and He owns the whole universe and everything in it, there is no limit to His supplies. We can ask the Father for what we need, in Jesus' name.

Have you heard of George Muller and his work with orphans? He opened his home to perhaps thousands of children over the years. He always prayed for their food, and oftentimes had no idea how it was going to be supplied. Even when there was no food visible, they'd gather 'round the table, bless the food "in absentia," and someone would always arrive with what they needed. They never missed a meal. George had faith in God's Word not only for himself but for others, and he certainly must have had a supernatural gift of faith for the work to which God had called him.

George asked and he expected to receive. "Expectation" is sitting down with your knife and fork and saying, "Thank You, Lord; I prayed, and here I am!" Richard Gorsuch, a commercial artist friend of ours, puts it this way: "Faith is taking a big frying pan and a camera with you when you go fishing."

Daily Bread Living

If you expect to be supplied with your needs "one day at a time," does that mean you should not make plans for the future? Not necessarily. You plan ahead, but you don't worry ahead! Jesus said it would be foolish for a king to go to battle without planning the campaign (Luke 14:31–32). You can live a day at a time, yet have a definite goal in view. From the beginning, Jesus planned to lay down His life for our sins and rise again for our salvation. Yet along the way, whether or not He knew where He would sleep at night, He wasn't anxious or in a hurry but lived in daily dependence on His Father. You, too, need to have plans, but also to have a "one-day-at-a-time" attitude knowing He will be with you every day. Often when I have too much to do and begin to feel under stress, I am relieved when I remember the principle of taking a day at a time. It helps me take a deep breath and relax.

Daily bread living will keep you from stress, especially when you're working to overcome personal problems. If you're fighting temptation, or a physical or psychological problem, God will bring you through each day to victory. Alcoholics Anonymous encourages people overcoming addictions to adopt this "one-day-at-a-time" attitude. You, too, can make it through this day with God's help not yielding to any addictive habit.

Bread from Heaven

God's spiritual bread is never like the bakery's day-old bread. The manna fell from heaven at night and was collected each morning, and so the children of Israel were sustained during their forty-year wilderness journey. The Scripture says the manna resembled the seed of the coriander plant, and was both tasty and nourishing (Exodus 16:31). The Israelites ground it each day to make flour for bread. But if they tried to save it over till the next day, it spoiled. The exception, which showed its supernatural source, was that once a week the manna lasted two days, so the Israelites could collect enough not to have to work on the Sabbath.

Jesus said,

> "Most assuredly, I say to you, Moses did not give you the bread from heaven, but My Father gives you the true bread from heaven. For the bread of God is He who comes down from heaven and gives life to the world. . . . I am the bread of life. He who comes to Me shall never hunger, and he who believes in Me shall never thirst. . . . Most assuredly, I say to you, he who believes in Me has everlasting life. . . . I am the living bread which came down from heaven. If anyone eats of this bread, he will live forever."
>
> John 6:32–33, 35, 47, 51

Here Jesus is using manna as a type of Himself. This means that we, too, must feed on Jesus Christ *each* day to receive living, fresh Bread, our spiritual food from heaven.

An Irish manuscript from the eleventh century reads, "Give us today for bread the Word of God from heaven."[3] Your spirit and soul receive "daily bread" as you feed on Jesus, the Bread of Life. How do you feed on the Word of God? You do this daily by practicing His presence in prayer; by sharing and listening reflectively through the Lord's Prayer and other prayers; by feeding on His Word; by receiving holy Communion (the Lord's Supper, the Eucharist, the Mass); by worship and praise; by enjoying fellowship with others in the Lord; by caring for those in need. Take inventory to see if you're feeding in these ways.

Just like any good father, God wants to give you food for your body, as well as supply all your other needs for your spirit and soul. If your body isn't taken care of, your inner person will be hindered in receiving from God. Says *The Interpreter's Bible*, "When we seek the mind of Christ, and pray in sincerity the prayer he taught, a change is wrought—bread for the body, bread for the family of mankind, bread for the soul."[4]

Prayer

"Give us today our daily bread . . ."

Dear Father God, You are the Creator of all things, the Provider for my daily bread. I can't earn it, but by grace You have given it to me because You love me. Thank You for taking care of me day after day.

Show me how to feed myself and those dear to me with the right kind of "bread" so they'll be strong and healthy physically, psychologically and spiritually. Help me daily make the right choices in food and drink, and not to overindulge in them or in the other good things You give me. Teach me how best to share my bread, both natural and spiritual, with the hungry.

Please feed my spirit and soul, and forgive me when I fail to take time to receive Your nourishment. Above all, thank You, dear Father, for sending the Bread of Heaven, Your Son, Jesus Christ, to earth to feed me.

I love You, Father, Jehovah-Jireh. Thank You for my daily bread and all it means.

Pause, reflect and praise.

9

And Forgive Us
Our Sins

In 1989 a prisoner wrote to me with this concern: "I've read the Lord's Prayer, and it says I'm not going to be forgiven until I forgive everybody! I'm so scared! Won't you and one of your friends please come and pray for me here in Texas?" Since Seattle is quite a distance from Texas, it wasn't possible for me to visit him personally. But I wrote him; and what I am about to share with you is the essence of my answer to him.

To understand this part of the Lord's Prayer you must distinguish between original *sin* and actual *sins*. Original sin was man's decision to mistrust and disobey God, which became the avenue for Satan to take over the earth resulting in total separation from God. The only possible way to redeem the situation was through Jesus' death and resurrection bringing us the cure—the new birth. Jesus defined sin this way: "And when He [the Holy Spirit] has come, He will convict the world of sin, and of righteousness, and of judgment: of sin, because they do not believe in Me . . ." (John 16:8–9). When you repent and receive Jesus Christ as your Savior and Lord, original sin and its effects are removed from you, because your spirit and God are now conjoined through the Holy Spirit.

Actual sins, on the other hand, are wrong things you do (sometimes daily) that unless repented of will separate you from fellowship with God and keep Him from being able to work in your soul. They will make you vulnerable to wrong choices and the enemy's fiery darts. They may not make you lose your salvation, but they will keep you from being aware of it and enjoying it, and your life will not make the kind of witness that draws others into the Kingdom.

A Beggar Becomes a Princess

On a spring day in 1988, I stopped to talk to a street person, a nineteen-year-old, sitting on the sidewalk in downtown Seattle with a sign stationed in front of her saying, "I need food, money and a job." I offered her half the sandwich I had just bought. I told her, "God loves you and wants you to have a happy and fulfilling life. He wants you to live like a princess!"

She looked interested and said, "I believe in God, but I have a question. Why are such terrible things going on in the world, if there is a God?"

I replied, "Dawn [I found that was her name], in the beginning this world wasn't a mess, it was a paradise. It went wrong when the first human beings decided to go against God's will and to rebel against His plan. They decided to obey a demonic king and turned the world over to him. This began a battle between two kingdoms, the Kingdom of light and the kingdom of darkness. The evil going on in this world is certainly not from God.

"God's solution was to allow His own Son, Jesus, to fight this greatest of all spiritual battles to gain the world and His people back from the leader of the evil kingdom. This led to the death of Jesus. Yet His death was not a defeat, because through it He conquered the evil king, plus his usurped kingdom, and not only that, but three days later Jesus came back from the dead. Jesus is now King of kings and Lord of lords. Through His death and resurrection He rescued the world and all who would believe in Him.

"There is still a clean-up war going on. Though the evil king, Satan, has been defeated he doesn't give up easily. Many people are still working for him. People are either in the Kingdom of light or the kingdom of darkness. They join God's side by accepting His Son.

"Have you ever asked Jesus Christ into your life, Dawn?"

She answered, "No, I haven't."

"Would you like to?" I inquired.

She looked up and said sincerely, "Yes, I would."

We joined hands, and I had the joy of introducing her to Jesus and seeing her come into the Kingdom of light.

I then told her, "Dawn, you now have the right to ask for help in the name of Jesus. This knowledge is the greatest gift I can give you. Scripture teaches that all power has been given to Jesus and you have the right to use His name for good in this world."

I gave her my small Bible, told her how to use it, asked how I could contact her and hugged her good-bye, just in time for my dentist appointment.

She's just starting her life with Jesus. Dawn's met the One who doesn't want her to be ashamed any longer; she is a newborn daughter of the King, and God wants her to live like one. (Next, she needs to receive the power of the Holy Spirit and join in fellowship with other believers.)

After I came back from the dentist I saw Dawn was no longer sitting on the sidewalk. My heart sang a little, as I felt the new life in her had already started working.

In this illustration I'm referring first of all to original sin, which was canceled for you when you came into the family of God. As a result, your spirit was made whole and joined to God, and your soul and body were saved spiritually, although they will need physical and psychological saving daily. Likewise, Dawn's original sin (her separation from God) was removed when she received Jesus Christ. Now to keep in right relationship with God and man she will need to bring her actual sins (wrongdoings) to Jesus day by day. This is true of all Christians.

Little Deaths or Little Resurrections?

When Jesus gave us the words *Forgive us our sins,* He was talking abut sins in the plural (actual sins). This deals with keeping our lives right daily. Remember this as we go on.

The prophet Isaiah defines sin very simply: "All we like sheep have gone astray [that's original sin]; we have turned, every one, to his own way [that's actual sins]; and the Lord has laid on Him the iniquity of us all" (53:6).

St. Augustine of Hippo wrote: "In the Gospel according to Matthew the Lord's Prayer seems to embrace seven petitions, three of which ask for eternal blessings, and the remaining four for temporal. . . . But when we say [in the last four petitions], [4] 'Give us this day our daily bread: [5] and forgive us our debts, as we forgive our debtors: [6] and lead us not into temptation, [7] but deliver us from evil,' who does not see that we ask for blessings that have reference to the wants of this present life?"[1]

So I think you and I, along with St. Augustine, have reason to believe that *Forgive us our sins* refers to forgiving the things we do wrong day by day, rather than having to deal regularly with original sin. Wouldn't it be awful to think that if a Christian was rushing to the emergency room of a hospital and was killed while driving ten miles over the speed limit, his breach of traffic laws might keep him out of heaven?

Paul distinguishes between soul—the psychological nature—and spirit—the new creation life (1 Thessalonians 5:23). I don't believe that Jesus in this part of the Lord's Prayer was speaking of sin of the spirit. That kind of sin would mean the person was either continuing to reject Jesus, or had become totally apostate by renouncing his or her relationship with the Savior until death. Rather, Jesus was speaking here of the daily (actual) sins of the soul.

In the Lord's Prayer, the Greek translation shows Jesus using two different words for sins. Matthew 6:12 uses *opheilema*, meaning "to be in debt to someone, to fail to give a person his or her due, not giving the good deserved." That to me means we should give credit to whomever credit is due; for instance, in the use of others' original ideas, like music or words for quotes, or giving one's due in the home or in the church. *Opheilema* is usually translated "debts," as in "forgive us our debts" (Matthew 6:12).[2]

In Luke 11:4, *hamartia* is used for sins: "And forgive us our sins [*hamartia*], for we also forgive every one who is indebted to us." Aristotle called it the "missing of virtue" out of defective knowledge, better known to us today as "missing the mark." It reminds me of Jesus' cry from the cross: "Father, forgive them, for they do not know what they do" (Luke 23:34). Yet according to the lexicon, the *hamartia* kind of sin can also mean sins with evil intent.[3]

When Dennis was speaking at a meeting one day he said, "Sins are actually 'little deaths.'" That was the first time I ever heard that idea and I was impressed with the truth of it. As I mulled it over the thought came to me, *Then repentances could be called "little resurrections," couldn't they?* Every time you sin, you experience a little death and every time you repent, you experience a little resurrection, so you'd better make sure you have more little resurrections than you do little deaths!

Daily Sins Erect Barriers

Notice that immediately following Jesus' model for prayer in Matthew 6:9–13, He repeats for emphasis the importance of forgiving, which is the subject of our next chapter: "For if you forgive men their trespasses, your heavenly Father will also forgive you. But if you do not forgive men their trespasses, neither will your Father forgive your trespasses" (verses 14–15). Sobering words, which we can now understand better as we go on in this study. Here Greek translations show Jesus using a third word for sins, *paraptomata. Strong's Concordance* explains its first meaning as "slipping from the right path unintentionally," but it can also mean "a willful transgression."

My prisoner friend needed to know that he must deal with actual sins (daily sins) he has not yet repented from. If original sin were forgiven only "as we forgive those who sin against us," it would make his salvation, and our salvation, most uncertain!

Jesus warns you (and me) not to live in daily sins. If you do, you'll erect barriers between you and God, so that you won't be aware of His presence or be able to be His close friend, sensitive to His guidance for your protection and blessing. Your spirit is safe, joined to the Lord (1 Corinthians 6:17), but unless you keep your account up-to-date, your soul will lose out on many of God's rewards in this life and in the next (1 Corinthians 3:12–15).

One of the major emotions we need to deal with is guilt. True guilt is caused by your sins and is taken care of only through repentance. We get rid of daily sins by repenting and confessing them, which we should do immediately or, at the very least, at the end of each day. "Let not the sun go down upon your wrath: neither give place to the devil" (Ephesians 4:26–27, KJV). First John 1:9 says, "If we confess our sins [*hamartia*], He is faithful and just to forgive us our sins and to cleanse us from all unrighteousness."

Praise be to God for "little resurrections" daily!

Prayer

"And forgive us our sins . . ."

Dear Abba Father, please forgive me from sins in thoughts, words and deeds; sins known and unknown to me at this time. *[Pause here if you have something you need to make right with God.]*

Thank You that as I let You heal my soul it gets easier to control the tendency to commit sins. David said, "He restores my soul; He leads me in the paths of righteousness. . ." and living right with You seems to come more easily in that order (Psalm 23:3). Please restore, resurrect, my soul, and as I allow You to do this I know You will lead me in right paths, safe paths.

Thank You that because You are so good and because I'm doing what the Holy Spirit shows me in my spirit and in Scripture, I can always live forgiven. It's a healthy life, and a happy one, too! Thank you, *Jehovah-Tsidkenu*, righteous Father. And thank You so much for Your Son, Jesus Christ, through whose righteousness alone I come to You.

Pause and reflect.

10
As We Forgive Those Who Sin Against Us

When General James Oglethorpe said to John Wesley, "I never forgive," Wesley answered, "Then I hope, sir, you never sin."[1]

God will forgive your soul's sins as you not only ask forgiveness for yourself, but forgive others their sins against you. You will receive the same measure as you give.

The Greek word for "forgive" in Matthew 6:12 is actually the past tense *ophekamen*. The verse could then be read, "And *forgive* us our sins, as we *forgave* those who sinned against us." That's a nice way to look at it because you're seeing it as done before it happens! Through Jesus' stripes you *are* and *were* healed; this includes your soul as well as your body, yet you must enter in to make it yours experientially. Then through God's provision and grace—and *only* through them—do you have the power to forgive. The meanings for the word *forgave* are "let go, sent away, canceled, remitted or pardoned."[2]

Jesus teaches us by example to forgive others *unconditionally*— that is, even before we are asked. He forgave from the cross, setting free you and me and whosoever will come to Him. *As you forgive, you set people free to come to you to be reconciled.*

Satan is the greatest hater. He teaches people *not* to forgive— to hold permanent grudges, to get even, to take revenge. God is the greatest Lover. He took your guilt and, through His Son, died in your place. You have the power to choose which one you want to be like, the hater or the Lover.

What If I Have Trouble Forgiving Others?

In the Christian faith we've been taught a lot about how to ask forgiveness for our own sins, and rightly so, as a first step. But we haven't often been taught about how to forgive *others*. Teaching in more than two hundred churches over the last twelve years, I've found this to be an immense need.

The ministry that helps people do this has been called by various names; some are: inner healing, inner wholeness, emotional healing or, more specifically, soul healing prayer. Lay people and clergy of many denominations who have been healed themselves are in turn helping others who have gotten stuck in their spiritual growth. It's something like breaking up logjams that block the flow of the Holy Spirit in people's lives. There is no set formula on how this is to happen, except that when we understand that our resurrected Lord Jesus is there in our yesterdays, then His loving presence and the insights He gives release us, healing our memories and emotions. As this happens, we are able to forgive on a new level. We can then obey Jesus' words and "forgive as we have been forgiven."

The "logjam" can come from present-day problems, but the foundation for it is very often found back in childhood, sometimes so far back one can't by himself get in touch with it because he or she can't remember it. Fortunately God is omniscient; in the words of Merrill C. Tenney, He "perfectly and eternally knows all things which can be known."[3] When asked, He will show you and those praying with you the exact location of where your problem began! I have seen this miracle happen hundreds of times and it is always amazing. I have observed that the people most responsive to prayer for inner healing are those who really want to be free, and especially those who are committed to a fellowship of God's people.

Doing the Work of Heaven

Assisting others to forgive is doing the work of heaven because it brings some heaven to earth. It's hard to forgive and let go. This is where prayer for emotional or memory healing comes in, because it helps us forgive in those particular situations totally and permanently. Let me give you a few examples.

Understanding Soft Rocks

Pat had just come off night duty from her nursing job and was waiting and dozing in her car before meeting with my friend and co-worker, Shirley Wilson, and me for prayer. A short time later as we met, Pat told us that while beginning to doze in the car she had had an inner vision of being hit by soft rocks that also appeared to be sharp. As she told us about it, she remembered nightmares she had had in her childhood of these same soft rocks bombarding her! It's not uncommon for the Holy Spirit to give the person being prayed with an inner vision or picture, to remind her of a dream or memory in childhood; this is the way He gently leads her (or him) to the key place that needs healing.

We asked if Pat had been called any negative names in child-hood. The kids in second grade had called her "Fatty Patty." We felt this was important because she was working on a needed weight loss and addiction to candy. We prayed about this, bind-ing and casting out the negative and painful effects of the name "Fatty Patty"—doing it in Jesus' name (see Matthew 18:18). Then we asked the Lord to give her a new name and a new memory. As we waited in prayer, Shirley felt that Jesus gave the name "Fabulous Patty" and then Pat knew He was urging her to hug the kids rather than chase them and hit them for calling her names. Next she saw all the kids lined up in front of her (as little Patty) and Jesus to get their hugs. She forgave the kids.

Let Pat tell more about it in her own words: "We still had not figured out what the soft rocks were, and Rita suggested they might be all the semi-kidding 'jokes' that were in fact painful and hurtful—especially with parent figures. It had already occurred to me when I read what I had written up [in preparation for this prayer time] about my parents' good and bad points, that Daddy's joking was not always a good point, though his attitude of hap-piness was.

"One specific thing that came to mind was Daddy's *always, always* saying, 'That's what they fatten hogs on,' when he passed me the corn. Rita and Shirley led me in prayer to cast out the name 'Piggy' and its effect on me. For the name 'Piggy' I was unable to hear a name replacement, but I saw myself beautiful, poised like a bride, in my long, old-fashioned calico dress. [This was the dress she had worn twelve years earlier, before her daugh-ter was born. She still has it and plans to be able to wear it again!]

"Shirley said that this picture was part of the new name: 'Fab-ulous Patty.' I also felt the Lord gave me the name from Scripture 'Child of God.' I forgave Daddy, through Jesus, and asked the Lord to relay this message of love to him in heaven.

112

"Knowing how much I joke and tease, I asked the Lord's forgiveness and broke any wrong generational ties between Daddy, me and my kids. I don't want to throw any soft rocks at my family!"

It became clear to the three of us that the soft rocks pertained to her father's words; he was always joking and kidding, with a kind of affection, but hidden within were cutting words. This soft rock image is an appropriate description for those who know its potential for hurt. A soft rock is something that appears soft but is really sharp and when it hits it cuts you. Obvious offenses, hard rocks such as the kids calling her names, also hurt but not as deeply because they are out in the open and therefore can be dealt with openly. Soft rocks work on the subconscious and wound from the inside; you can't detect them unless you get insight such as the Holy Spirit gave us that day.

Pat has now lost 45 pounds and is looking more glamorous every day! We met with her a number of times to complete the things she wanted to pray about. She's now praying with others and seeing them helped and healed.

Healed from Masculine Disapproval

A woman in her late twenties, whom I'll call Lou, wanted prayer for one specific memory when she was twelve and was embarrassed in front of her sixth-grade class. A boy nominated her for school council. When the votes were counted, there was only one vote for her. That was humiliating enough, but then her "friend" revealed to the class that he had not voted for her either. He made public the fact that Lou had cast this only vote for herself. To make matters even worse, another boy she was sure would vote for her didn't, and the teacher, a father figure and someone she expected support from, did nothing to help her during or after her embarrassment.

My prayer partner and I prayed with her and waited quietly to see how the Holy Spirit would minister to her. She looked back over the circumstances of the painful memory and told us she could feel Jesus put His hand on her shoulder. Then she heard Him say, *I voted for you!* This was better than having the whole class vote for her! It was a special moment of healing and brought tears of release.

We again waited because we felt Jesus would affirm her as a woman and as a worthy person. Lou heard Him call her *a queen!* We asked her if she could see any queenly qualities in herself. It took a little time but she realized she had confidence, leadership ability and competency.

When it came time to forgive those three males who had hurt her, she didn't find it hard because, as she said, "It's not as hard for a queen to forgive." We asked Jesus to give her His true masculine love and acceptance, filling the gap deep within her being.

Pornography Addiction Healed

A Christian man, whom I'll call Russell, was addicted to pornography for six years and had spent great amounts of money on his habit. He had no idea why he was compelled this way, but as we prayed the key to his bondage was revealed. Russell's parents were divorced when he was about three years of age. His father left and his mother had to work away from home. All of a sudden *he had lost both parents.*

In our society we are too often taught that "love is sex and sex is love." There is no doubt that the sexual embrace is a part of a healthy marriage relationship, but self-giving love goes far beyond this. While trying to regain his childhood losses, Russell turned to illicit sexual stimulation through pornography, misinterpreting those feelings as love. Walking through those childhood traumas with Jesus brought healing love to his past, and showed him what real love is.

With God's love enabling him, he forgave his parents from the deep emotions of his past childhood memories. An infant doesn't understand divorce or where Daddy and/or Mother went. He may simply feel rejection and that something must be wrong with him or this wouldn't have happened. Those wounds may affect a person all of his or her life unless they are dealt with and healed.

Strong deliverance prayers were needed, too, because misbehavior had left his soul and body vulnerable to demonic invasion. At the end of our prayer time we were joyful but also knew we had been in a spiritual battle. We gave Russell instructions on how to keep his healing and recommended further prayer, for his soul's needs were deep. In dealing with addictions such as this, it is highly recommended that deliverance prayers be coupled with soul healing prayers for total restoration.

We gave him these following steps if in his recovery process he were to slip again:

1. Ask and receive God's forgiveness. (Do this in whatever way his church recommends.)

2. Forgive himself. (May need prayer from others to help here.)

3. In Jesus' name and blood, cast away any evil spirits he had given ground to, such as unclean spirits or spirits of lust (Matthew 10:1; Luke 10:19–20).

4. Ask the Holy Spirit to fill those areas of his soul that have been cleansed, and to fill his life to the fullest measure possible.

5. Get more soul healing prayer help through experienced Christians or, if knowledgeable enough himself, pray for his own

inner healing and look for keys of vulnerability connected with any recent circumstances in which he was treated unkindly or put down in some way. See if these keys link up with an unhealed memory (or memories) in his childhood. Forgive anyone he needs to in the past and present.

6. Realize God's love by reading Scripture and books that reflect this, and by participating frequently in a loving Christian fellowship.

7. Stay away from the places and people who tempt him.

These steps would be helpful to anyone with any addiction, whether it be illicit sex, alcohol, drugs, gambling or kleptomania, to name a few.

There are those who have small problems and those who have big problems. But whatever their size, Jesus, by the Holy Spirit, is teaching the Body of Christ these days how to pray so He can reach deep into our emotions, memories and subconscious minds. Once we let Him, He will free us from the bondages of both the past and present—helping us forgive those who have hurt us, receive healing from the hurts sustained in a fallen world, and "loose" the burdens of fear, anger, depression and other emotions that debilitate us.

Forgiveness

The dictionary defines *forgiveness* this way: "To cease to feel resentment against (an offender), to give up resentment of or claim to requital for (an insult)."[4]

Martin Luther King's father, speaking at a Christian conference, said, "No one has the power to make me hate." He said this even though his wife had been shot while he looked on helplessly, and on the heels of his son's assassination. Only God

116

could give him this depth of forgiveness—unconditional forgiveness, God's kind of forgiveness.

If you don't forgive, you give your enemy power over you. To forgive someone does not mean you agree with his wrong behavior, or that you need to make him your best friend, or that you even have to particularly like him or her. It just means you are choosing to follow Jesus, let the hurt go and walk in God's peace and wholeness. Though you may not choose to make this person a close friend here on earth—nor would this perhaps be best for you or your family—it does mean that if that person were the first one to greet you as you were about to enter into heaven, you would accept his or her love and not choose to go the other direction!

Two Important Ways to Forgive

I've found there are two important ways to forgive. First, you must forgive everyone *at the level of your will* every day if you are going to walk in God's protection and fellowship. Second, you need to forgive *at the level of your emotions*. This kind of forgiveness may not be realized immediately, but may have to be worked on for a period of time.

How do you forgive at the level of the will? You choose to forgive whether or not you *feel* like it. Jesus commanded us to love and forgive, which means we have the ability to do it. Forgiveness is above all a choice, something we decide to do. With God's help you can do it. Some of us were taught as children that forgiving meant accepting what was being done to us no matter how bad it was. That would keep us in the bondage of unforgiveness for sure! Forgiving is not saying to the persons who hurt us, "You were right"; rather, it is saying in essence, "You did wrong, but I choose to forgive you regardless." Forgiveness is the refusal to hold ill will toward someone else for what he or she did or didn't do. It means giving up resentment, bitterness, complaining or plans to get even—and unloading that heavy backpack at the foot of the cross! This includes forgiving your own self, too, because if you don't love and forgive yourself, you won't be able to reach out with love and forgiveness to others.

It's O.K. to admit to God that this is particularly hard to do. He knows your heart so you might as well "tell it like it is!" You might say something like, "Dear Father, I find it hard to forgive Jackie [or Jack] for what she [he] did to me. I'm still angry about it, but I give the anger to You. Part of me [the soul] doesn't want to forgive, but part of me [the spirit] does. Though I don't want to forgive, I *want* to want to, so I choose to obey You and forgive, right now, and let You deal with any resentment, bitterness or revenge that I still feel. In Jesus' name."

Sometimes you forgive with the will and yet the bad memory lingers on, causing you to have to continue to forgive with the will over and over again. You would like to be totally free, but like a sore tooth, the memory still hurts when you chew on it. You may find that you're talking to a number of people about the hurt, or thinking about it a lot. You can't seem to get it off your mind. If you've forgiven and forgiven and yet the hurt is still inside, you need to take the next step.

How do you forgive from the level of the emotions? This is a time when you should seek help from others. Find a team of two or three prayer counselors versed in inner healing prayer to meet with you and pray through this hurtful memory. Prayer sessions may be something like those mentioned earlier with Pat, Lou and Russell, though God is so creative that what He does is always a little different. When your memory has been healed, then you can forgive the person easily from the level of your emotions.

Since emotional wounds are from the past, it helps to heal

them when you speak forgiveness from that time frame. For instance, Pat's memory with her classmates took place when she was seven, so feeling and/or picturing herself as the child, Patty, she said something like the following: "Dear Lord, please tell the kids in my class: I forgive you for [name the hurt] and I won't hold this against you any longer. What you did was painful, but I let the pain go. I won't hold onto it any longer. You truly didn't know what you were doing [speaking from God's viewpoint]. Jesus has healed me and set me free. In His name I pray."

Other related memories may surface as you pray about this one. Simply follow the Holy Spirit's leading to wholeness. The physically or sexually abused person will find soul (inner) healing prayer and this second step of forgiveness especially helpful, but will need the support of an experienced prayer team. Eventually not only will you be able to forgive on both levels, but your emotions and memories will be totally free from the results of others sins against you, whether they were large or small.

I'd like to quote some concluding thoughts on these two ways of forgiving from my book *Making Peace with Your Inner Child:* ". . . The first is forgiving on the level of your relationship with God. The second is forgiving on the level of your relationship with man (if you cannot verbalize this forgiveness it shows you still have emotional blocks). The first cleanses you in your relationship to God. The second releases you in your relationship to people. . . . One is forgiving on the level of your spirit, your will being the doorway from soul to spirit. The second is forgiving from the level of your soul (emotions, memory, and will)."[5]

Inner Wholeness, Forgiveness and the Lord's Prayer

Isaiah prophesied the coming of Jesus' healing ministry when he said,

"The Spirit of the Lord God is upon Me, because the Lord
has anointed Me to preach good tidings to the poor; He has
sent Me to heal the brokenhearted, to proclaim liberty to
the captives, and the opening of the prison to those who
are bound . . . to comfort all who mourn, to console
those who mourn in Zion, to give them beauty for ashes,
the oil of joy for mourning, the garment of praise for the
spirit of heaviness."

Isaiah 61:1, 3

God has called us all in some way to carry on His ministry. It's
been an exciting and challenging time since 1977 when I was
thrust into this work of praying for the broken in heart and soul.
I guess I was one of the pioneers. (You can tell a pioneer by the
buckshot holes in his clothes!)

One result of praying with people for soul healing is that I can
see steps of healing in various portions of Scripture, and one that
has become more and more clear to me is the Lord's Prayer itself.
I hadn't realized before I entered this ministry the amount of
inner wholeness that could come through meditating on the
Lord's Prayer, nor had I heard it taught this way. Near the end of
chapter 13, I'll give you these steps as they were clarified even
further while writing this book. The Lord's Prayer, in itself,
when used as Jesus must have intended, will bring you much
healing. It will help you be a one-hundred-percent forgiver.

As you forgive those who have sinned against you, you are
also forgiven. You can't afford to carry around a trash can of
unforgiveness containing things like a friend's betrayal, a continuing resentment you have for a person, participating in an
office or family feud or holding onto the hurts of your childhood.
Unforgiveness for things such as these separates your conscious
self from God, and makes others who live around you miserable,

too. And unforgiveness can block all kinds of blessings God wants to give you, such as the empowering of the Holy Spirit, physical healing, peace that passes understanding, prosperity in general, being successful in your chosen field and feeling good about yourself.

I don't believe God wants us to live in fear of losing our salvation, nor does He, on the other hand, want us to live carelessly regarding our relationships with others. That's why Jesus gave us these words of caution to draw us to live as He lived. If we pray the Lord's Prayer daily, from our hearts, and live as He shows us to, we will have done our part to walk in forgiveness to the best of our ability. This is all God asks of us.

I believe for these reasons, and others I'm sure, our Lord Jesus put this forgiveness challenge in the prayer He taught *all* His disciples to pray.

Prayer:

"As we forgive those who sin against us . . ."

Dear Father, I will thank You forever for sending Your Son, Jesus, to forgive me and show me how to forgive. I can't do it in my own strength, but I allow You to forgive in me and through me. Teach me to love and forgive unconditionally.

Thank You that You don't violate my free will. Father God, I give You permission to go to any level within me, to heal, cleanse and restore according to Your truth. I ask You to be Lord of my subconscious as well as the rest of my life. Reveal to me any unforgiveness that I'm not aware of. I choose this day to follow Your Son, Jesus, my Lord, and to be a one-hundred-percent forgiver.

Lord, as Your Son prayed from the cross for His enemies, I pray for all those who have hurt me intentionally or unintentionally: Father, "forgive them for they know not what they do." *[Pause, as you hear Jesus saying this to each person, and also release that person and your hurtful memories to Him.]* I choose to forgive them and set them free now from my judgment, and I place them in Your loving care. Thank You that my emotions and memories are being healed as I follow You, dear Father.

And though I love so much to think of You as "my Father," help me remember you are also "our Father"; help me learn how to accept Your other kids. I pray all this through Jesus Christ, Your Son.

Pause and reflect.

11
Lead Us Not into Temptation

Why does Jesus want you to pray that the Father will not lead you into temptation? Why would He tell you to pray such a prayer? Is God working with Satan, as some have taught, tempting us "for our own good"? Would Jesus lead His own family into temptation?

First, let us try to define what is meant by the word *temptation*. The Greek here is *peirasmos,* which the lexicon says means a test or a trial, a temptation, an enticement to sin. Webster's first definition of *tempt* is to "entice to do wrong by promise of pleasure or gain." The authoritative *Theological Dictionary of the New Testament* (Kittel and Friedrich) points out that from very early times this petition in the Lord's Prayer was seen as a request for God's protection *against* temptation.[1] And this is the way it is interpreted in Luther's Smaller Catechism: "That the devil, the world, and our flesh may not deceive . . . us." *The*

Interpreter's Bible says, "The word rendered temptation might mean 'trial' or 'persecution,' but the petition is usually taken as a request that God will remove occasions of sin or the evil impulse which promotes sin."[2] The reference in the *Theological Dictionary of the New Testament* says further, "The petition is not related to Psalm 139:23, which asks God to try the heart. If it were, it would have to be the direct opposite: Lead us into temptation."[3]

What Does Jesus Say About Temptation?

Let's let Jesus Himself answer the question posed earlier. The last words He spoke to His disciples before His arrest and crucifixion were given in the midst of His agonized prayers to the Father from the Mount of Olives: "Pray that you will not fall into temptation" (Luke 22:40, NIV). Luke describes how the disciples tried to support Him, but fell asleep in their exhaustion and sorrow while waiting for Jesus. They were awakened by His speaking to them again: "Rise and pray that you may not enter into temptation" (Luke 22:46, RSV).

Matthew's record of Jesus' words is similar: "Watch and pray, lest you enter into temptation. The spirit indeed is willing, but the flesh is weak" (Matthew 26:41). The Greek word use here for "flesh" is *sarx,* and in this place it refers to "human or mortal nature,"[4] that is, to the soul (*psyche*) and the body (*soma*).

Jesus was concerned about what would happen to the faith of His chosen after He allowed Himself to be killed; He was also concerned about those who would come into the faith throughout history as a result of their witness. He knew some things were about to happen to Him that the disciples wouldn't understand until after His death and until they could see Him again in His resurrection body, when He would breathe the life of His Holy

Spirit into their spirits. He knew that even then they wouldn't fully understand until their Pentecost (Acts 1:6–7).

Those words of Jesus in Gethsemane are also for us, His modern disciples. He's saying two things:

1. Ask God to keep you from being tempted to say and do wrong things through the deception of Satan;

2. Be on the alert and pray frequently, as it is fellowship with God that will keep you from falling into temptation.

In the Lord's Prayer you're praying in agreement with God when you pray against being tempted. Jesus shows that a person who prays will be protected and ready to resist temptation when it comes. Prayer is a primary way to keep you from *beginning* to yield. And resisting the initial temptation is easier than getting out of a situation.

He wants you to know from this phrase of the prayer that He is *not* the author of temptation. If you think the temptation in your life is from God, you may passively accept it, and be defeated by it.

Jesus won't lead you into temptation; He will lead you *out* of temptation. John called Him "Good Shepherd" three times in chapter 10, so that means He is the good, good, good Shepherd! He loves and tenderly cares for His sheep. I can't imagine a good shepherd leading his sheep to the mouth of a wolves' den, enticing them to see if they're foolish enough to wander in and be eaten! No, the sheep who keep close to a true shepherd are protected by the club he uses to *beat off* the wolves.

Further good news is that Jesus is praying for you in heaven. He is not only the Good Shepherd, but also the great High Priest who intercedes for His beloved family (see Hebrews 7:24–25; 9:24). The Amplified New Testament says it best: ". . . For He (God) Himself has said, I will not in any way fail you *nor* give you up *nor* leave you without support. [I will] not, [I will] not,

[I will] not in any degree leave you helpless, *nor* forsake *nor* let [you] down, [relax My hold on you].—Assuredly not!'' (Hebrews 13:5; also see Joshua 1:5). I like that.

When Jesus taught this part of the prayer, He may have been thinking about His own temptation in the wilderness. He did not want His disciples to experience anything like what He went through. He knows our weakness and most likely prayed not only for Himself during His forty-day wilderness battle, which we call "the great temptation," but for you and me as well. "For we do not have a High Priest who cannot sympathize with our weaknesses, but was in all points tempted as we are, yet without sin" (Hebrews 4:15). He won the battle with the tempter not only for Himself but for us!

We also saw in chapter 4 how God the Father is called our "Good Shepherd," Jehovah-Roi. His Son, Jesus, has learned shepherding skills from His Father, and the Holy Spirit leads us as He looks to the Son.

So, in the Lord's Prayer we need to realize that we're praying *against* being tempted.

Protection from the Tempter

Who is the tempter anyway? Jesus Christ Himself and the apostle Paul both identify the tempter as Satan (see Matthew 4:10 and 1 Corinthians 7:5).

How does he work? About our Lord's great temptation Matthew records that Satan tempted Jesus to doubt His relationship to God: "If You are the Son of God" was his opening statement (Matthew 4:3). Satan also said this at the beginning of his second shot at Jesus; this attempt to make Jesus question His own authority was meant to weaken Him in the fight. He wants to weaken us as well by getting us to believe that our relationship with God is suspect.

Isn't it just like Satan, who is the deceiver and the father of lies, to so twist the truth that he can get Christians to believe that God is the tempter rather than himself? Diabolically clever! Author Charles Capps says, "Satan's greatest tool is deception. If he can deceive you into believing whatever [evil] comes to you is from God, you will not resist it."[5]

Satan is the tempter and God is not working with or through him in any way, shape or form! Satan is the archenemy of God. He is the prince of darkness, and the Scriptures say that there is no darkness in God at all. "Be ye not unequally yoked together with unbelievers: for . . . what communion hath light with darkness?" (2 Corinthians 6:14, KJV). "This then is the message which we have heard of him, and declare unto you, that God is light, and in him is no darkness at all" (1 John 1:5, KJV).

Satan is the *defeated* enemy ever since Calvary, but he hasn't given up yet. In Luke 10:18 Jesus states that He saw Satan fall from heaven. Thus I believe that Satan, the fallen archangel, has been ousted from heaven permanently and cannot stand before God's throne and accuse us—as he did Job—anymore (Luke 10:18). He is still, however, the attacker and the accuser of the brethren, but now he does it *on earth* and especially enjoys working through Christians who major in finding faults with and accusing one another.

But nothing delights him more than tempting Christians into accusing God for the very things Satan himself has done. Capps calls John 10:10 the "balance wheel of the Bible."[6] Here Jesus says, "The thief does not come except to steal, and to kill, and to destroy. I have come that they may have life, and that they may have it more abundantly." Very clearly Jesus says evil does not come from God. We must let the Bible be its own commentary, and look at all Scripture through the eyes of Jesus who in His own Person reveals to us what God is like. He is, as Hebrews says, the "express image" of the Father.

Paul says to the Corinthians that we have received the Spirit of God so that we can understand the things given to us from God. We speak these truths not with man's wisdom but through the teaching of the Holy Spirit, "comparing spiritual things with spiritual" (1 Corinthians 2:13). Those taking a proof-text approach could be confused on how to pray about temptation.

To see what temptation is like, let's return to Jesus' wilderness experience and see how Satan tempted Jesus. After attacking His relationship with His Father, as mentioned earlier, he tried to get Jesus to misuse supernatural gifts for His own ends, commanding Him to make bread out of stones. This temptation must have been selected especially because of Jesus' forty-day fast. Jesus would never perform a miracle for show, however, but only to help those in need.

The second temptation was to get Jesus to jump from the top of the Temple, supposedly again to prove His divinity by the angels' catching Him in their hands. Satan tried hard to convince Jesus to make this suicidal jump from the very Temple of God, but Jesus was secure in His relationship with His Father and was not going to make a sideshow of His power.

In the third temptation, Satan, who is presently only the usurper of man's dominion, wanted Jesus to bow down to him as if he were God. This was always Satan's big thing, to want to be God, and even though he was removed from heaven because of his rebellion he has never given up on it. He promised Jesus great earthly power over men and must have had the authority to give it, since Jesus did not challenge the validity of his offer. This "would-be" power had a pricetag we don't even want to imagine. And this time, before dispensing with the temptation, Jesus commanded the tempter to leave.

It's good to remember that Jesus didn't chitchat with Satan, but countered each temptation with Scripture alone.

And it's interesting to note that all of Jesus' sword-like Scriptures were taken from one book of the Old Testament— Deuteronomy (8:3, 6:16 and 6:13–14; also see 5:7–15). I had the fun of thinking I had discovered this myself in 1984 when writing an article for our teaching letter, but I found later that Finis Dake had discovered it years before! At any rate, with just a few words even from one book of the Bible, Jesus laid Satan low, and you can do the same.

To do spiritual battle, remember James' words: "Submit yourselves therefore to God. Resist the devil, and he will flee from you" (4:7, KJV). You, too, can use Scripture, as Jesus did, and then end with, "Get away from me, Satan, in Jesus' name!" and he has to go!

Temptation is not sin; every one of us has had tempting thoughts. It's what you do with those thoughts that causes you either to fall into sin or to win over it. Clarke gives the process of temptation like this: "1st. A simple evil thought. 2ndly. A strong imagination, or impression made on the imagination, by the thing to which we are tempted. 3dly. Delight in viewing it. 4thly. Consent of the will to perform it."[7] Jesus' temptation had greater ramifications than any other person's ever would in the history of the world, because His victory or failure would affect all mankind. Jesus' victory was won for you, so you also can walk free from the tempter's influence.

An Unsuspected Way of Temptation

Jesus' half-brother James says in his epistle in the New Testament, "Let no man say when he is tempted, I am tempted of

129

God: for God cannot be tempted with evil, neither tempteth he any man; but every man is tempted, when he is drawn away of his own lust, and enticed'' (James 1:13–14, KJV).

Here again the epistle of James says that God does not tempt. James does indicate, though, that our own weaknesses can make us vulnerable. *Temptation often comes from our own unhealed souls.* This is why it's important to seek healing for emotional wounds.

I've noticed, for example, in prayer and counseling, that women who were not given proper affection by their fathers can be sexually vulnerable; often they go from man to man for the physical love and verbal affirmation they missed in childhood. I've seen the same thing with men who lacked their mothers' love; they go from woman to woman trying to fill the empty places.

Does this topic touch a place within you? Then how do you fill the gaps in your childhood so you aren't "enticed," as James put it? You need to talk about your pain with a trusted person (working in prayer teams of two is preferable) who knows how to pray for soul healing, and ask Jesus to show you what needs His touch. Ask God to help you get in contact with repressed pain. Give that secret pain to Him. Walk through your hurtful memories with Jesus, allowing Him to be Lord of your past. With this kind of prayer, your childhood experiences with your father or mother, or with others, can be healed. Then you will be able to forgive them from your past memories as well as from the present.

Some Important Distinctions

Temptation, tribulation and testing are three different things. I've mentioned that *temptation* is being enticed to evil. *Tribula-*

tion is defined in the dictionary as "distress or suffering resulting from oppression or persecution." The Greek word is *thlipsis* and its first meaning is "distress caused by outward circumstances."

Both temptations and tribulations come from living in a world that's away from God, and is still being controlled by the enemy. They will come to you in various ways as they do to all God's people, but remember, they are not sent to you by your Father, or by His Son, Jesus. Jesus said specifically, "In this world you will have trouble, but cheer up, and don't be afraid; I have overcome the world!" (John 16:33, literal translation from the Greek).

If you're going to pray effectively you need to pray with faith; but how can you do that if you aren't sure whether or not it is God who is leading you into the temptation?

Testing is another matter. It has been defined as "a basis for evaluation." Now God does test, but not through disaster, sickness, accidents and tragedy. God tests us like a good teacher: He's not trying to flunk us, but wants to train us *to do the very best job for our welfare and our joy,* as well as *to build His Kingdom.* If it's a test from God, it won't "steal, kill or destroy."

I remember one of the tests God allowed me to have in 1961, the year after I had been released in the Spirit. At a retreat I attended, a woman came to me for prayer, but I was soon to find she really needed deliverance. The three women there with me were even less experienced than I was.

During the first moments of prayer the woman began to manifest the spirits troubling her. She began singing mockingly, "Jesus loves me, this I know," while she waved her hands like a hula dancer, her eyes big as saucers! I didn't need a whole lot of discernment to know where her behavior came from! There were no ministers or other leaders anywhere around, so I had to trust Jesus in me to do the work. In desperation I looked to Him, asking His direction step by step, and the woman was set free within four or five minutes of prayer.[8] Later that night she was gloriously filled with the Holy Spirit. I grew a lot that day!

To check whether something is a test from God or a temptation from yourself or the enemy, ask yourself, "Where did this come from: God, my renewed spirit, my unhealed soul or the enemy?" Then think about it. If it's from God or your spirit, it will be in agreement with what a loving, kind shepherd or trustworthy teacher would do. If it's from a part of your soul that is wounded or if it's from the enemy, it will be more like what a tyrannical or sadistic shepherd or teacher would do.

Jesus knew the weakness of humanity, and that you and I would need to pray for strength not to fall into temptation. Remember when you pray, "Lead me not into temptation," it means something like, "Thank You, Lord, that You do *not* lead me into temptation." Knowing these things, you realize without a shadow of a doubt that such freedom is His perfect will for you.

Prayer

"Lead us not into temptation . . ."

Father God and Lord Jesus, how can I ever thank You for all You've done for me? I am eternally indebted to You. Thank You that You have won the major battle, even though there are still scrimmages to be fought until by the power of the Holy Spirit this earth is brought under Your total loving rule.

Thank You, Father, for sending Jesus to be my good Shepherd, always calling to me, and nearby to guide me to safety. Savior, my Shepherd, I ask You to lead me. Show me the way. The world is so big and there are so many decisions to be made. Help me more and more to be able to discern and hear Your voice. Help me to keep the sword of Your Word ever at my side.

And good Lord, Good Shepherd, lead me out of temptation; lead me away from temptation before I can get involved in it. Help me to be so in tune with the Holy Spirit's leading that I will run from evil and walk in joyful obedience with You. Heal my soul so that I won't be vulnerable to temptation. *[If you know of weak areas in your soul offer them to God for healing at this point. Ask Jesus to lead you to the exact time and place where the problem got started, and heal you from there.]*

Thank You for being *Jehovah-Roi,* my Shepherd, and thank You, Father, for preparing and gently testing me like a loving Teacher, so I can grow. I love You, Father; I love You, Lord.

Pause and reflect.

12
But Deliver Us from Evil

During the first World War my father, William Harvey Reed, was in the ambulance corps of the Army. As he brought in the dead and wounded he was fully aware that there was an enemy out there. If anyone had tried to convince him that there really wasn't, that he was only imagining things, he would have said something like, "You're greatly mistaken, my friend; I know there's an enemy, because I've seen his destructive evidence! I've heard his artillery whizzing by my head."

Ephesians 6:12 tells us as followers of Jesus that our enemy is not made of flesh and blood as enemies in warfare normally are. This fact confuses many Christians because we tend to believe more easily what we can see. Our warfare is with a spiritual enemy, one we can't see except with eyes of the spirit, but the evidence that he exists cannot be doubted. When the wounded lie around us, it's obvious that there's a war going on.

If we're not in a war, Paul's writings to the Ephesians would not have warned Christians in the early Church and down to the present to put on their armor. The swords, spears, maces, bows and arrows used in those days are rather foreign to this day of missiles, chemical warfare and nuclear bombs, against which individual armor cannot much protect us. *Webster's New Collegiate Dictionary* says armor is a defensive covering for the body for use in combat. It shows a picture of fourteen pieces of armor to cover the soldier's entire body. Though the use of personal armor in warfare may be outdated, the message it gives is certainly *not* out of date. (We'll talk about this in more detail later in the chapter.)

Another way to look at our spiritual warfare comes from a point I mentioned earlier. Jesus has won the battle for us by His victorious death and resurrection, but there's still a lot of mopping up to be done. The enemy's army, Satan and his fallen angels, has had plenty of centuries to dig in and fight; it isn't such a simple thing to expel them, and so the guerrilla warfare goes on.

When you became a Christian you joined God's army. When you were empowered with the Holy Spirit you were no longer on reserve duty but were put on active duty. When you walk in that power and begin to bring others to the saving knowledge of Jesus and on into the fullness of the Holy Spirit, it threatens the enemy forces. When you help set people free from cultic beliefs and occult teachings, and command evil spirits to leave, as Jesus told you to do, the dark kingdom trembles. When you love and forgive others, it disgusts him. And when you minister in soul healing prayer—helping heal the wounded so they can live and love again, so they can actually feel God's love and forgive everyone in the past, present and future—this is especially offensive to the enemy.

When you do these things, you're not only sitting in the barracks studying your Soldier's Manual, but you're also out doing what the Book says. You're moving out onto the front lines, where your life will make a difference in the reclaiming of God's world.[1]

The concluding part of the Lord's Prayer is about your own release and your helping others to be set free, too. *Clarke's Commentary* points out that the words from the Lord's Prayer as presented in the King James Version, "Deliver us from evil," are an inadequate translation of the Greek. It says literally, "Deliver us from the wicked one."[2] Most modern versions translate it this way, or as, "Deliver us from the evil one."[3] This does seem to be the most logical rendering of the words, although it may also validly be translated, "Rescue us from the evil"—or literally, "Drag us away from the evil."

The Greek translated *Deliver us* is "a very expressive word—break our chains, and loose our bands—snatch, pluck us from the evil, and its calamitous issue," says Adam Clarke.[4]

God has come to rescue us *from evil,* and *from the evil one.* I think both renditions have meaning. He has come to break our bondages and set us free from those with wicked intentions, but the worst of all is the enemy himself.

First John 3:8 says, "The reason the Son of God was made manifest (visible) was to undo (destroy, loosen and dissolve) the works the devil [has done]" (AMPLIFIED). Jesus didn't come to use the enemy to whip us into shape! He came *to destroy him and everything he was and is doing.*

Jesus knows how to save us from evil. At the end of His forty-day fast in the wilderness, at the beginning of His ministry, He sent Satan away defeated. Jesus demonstrated the greatest victory of all when He died and rose from the dead, and won the "title deed" to the whole earth back from the enemy. Though Satan doesn't want to acknowledge that victory or give up the battle for men s lives, Jesus is Victor and His followers can walk in His victory

No Further Wilderness Experience Necessary

Some folks would say, "Jesus is our great example, and we see that immediately after being baptized He was empowered by the Spirit, and then *the Holy Spirit* led Him into the wilderness to be tempted (Luke 4:1–14). That must mean God is going to lead us into a wilderness experience, too."

No, I don't believe that at all. Because of what Jesus did for you, you don't have to fast forty days and nights to have victory, any more than you have to be crucified in order to have eternal life! Jesus is the Messiah; I'm not, and you're not! You can't redo the work He did. He finished it. Jesus said from the cross, "It is finished!" At times you will need to do spiritual warfare, and that may sometimes include fasting, but you'll do it from a position of victory.

Many Christians, when newly empowered and rejoicing in the Holy Spirit, detect the evil one and his direct influence for the first time, because their spiritual discernment has been heightened. The enemy is also more aware of *them*. Yet this is not to our hurt, but helps us know how to "set captives free"—one of the major works we are to do (Isaiah 61:1, 3; Mark 16:17).

It's been said, "If you're going in the same direction as the enemy you won't run into him, but if you're going in the opposite direction you will at some point come across him." But I would add, you certainly won't continue in his company!

In 1959 I lived in Newark, New Jersey, where I worked with children from multiracial backgrounds who were emotionally damaged. When I had free time I liked to go into New York City to enjoy musicals like "My Fair Lady," visit beautiful churches and in general see the sights. At one point I thought it would be fun to take voice lessons in Manhattan, so I found an instructor and began lessons. He played the piano well enough to accompany me, but he should have been giving me homework, vocalizations and so forth, and he obviously had no such plan. After three or four lessons, he told me a photographer would be coming next time, and wondered if I would like to have my picture in a magazine. He wanted the caption to say I was a "singer going to Hollywood."

Although I was only a nominal Christian at the time, I still heard a warning bell inside. This man wanted me to lie, and have it put into print! I made no response one way or the other, but determined then and there that that would be the last time he'd see me! I've since then wondered what kind of scheme he had going. I could have disappeared quite easily in the big city. I'm glad I had a mother who knew how to pray and intercede in the Spirit. I was delivered from dangerous situations in my youth, not just this time but many times, which I can now see much more clearly in retrospect.

You Are Equipped
with the Whole Armor of God

During my daily prayers, when I come to the final words of the Lord's Prayer, "Deliver us from evil," and before I give thanks in the concluding doxology, "For thine is the kingdom. . . ," I like to go through the armor of God passages found in Ephesians 6:13–18 to make sure I've put it on. My spirit, where Jesus dwells, is already fully protected, but my soul needs to be reminded of the battle by putting on and consciously appropriating what God has provided for me. It is vitally important for you, too, to know how to protect yourself and teach your family to do so. If the evil one can't get under your guard he will work on those closest to you, which can hurt not only them but you. The enemy isn't polite, nor does he play fair.

First look at verses ten through twelve, preceding the list of armor, which give helpful preliminary information:

a. Your strength is in the Lord and His power, not in your own abilities.

b. You're to put on the *whole* armor, not just part of it.

c. Paul tells us the enemy is "wily" or clever, so you need to be prepared for that.

d. Since the enemy has well-organized troops, you can't afford to be sloppy and undisciplined.

e. Three times in these verses we're told to stand against the enemy forces. Scripture doesn't say you're to sit down because it's all over, but stand and actively resist him. Fortunately, you're not always in active war. You'll have time to eat, rest, enjoy recreation, but you need to *live prepared*.

Now let's look at these seven pieces of armor.

The Belt of Truth

This is listed first, because truth encircling the center of your being is your greatest support. You're told to gird yourself with truth. "Gird one's loins" in *Webster's Dictionary* means "to prepare for action: muster up one's resources." A fitting place to begin. Just as the girdle gives support physically, so truth gives support spiritually.

In describing the area called *loins Webster's* again says it means "the upper and lower abdominal regions and the region about the hips, the pubic region, the generative organs." Historically and biblically, this is one of the most susceptible parts of the human body to the tempter. The enemy loves to get a hook into our sexuality if he can. This is another reason why the Holy Spirit listed this piece of armor first. You need to pray for protection over this vulnerable part of your body. Isaiah when prophesying about the coming of Jesus said, "And righteousness shall be the girdle [or belt] of his loins, and faithfulness the girdle of his reins" (11:5, KJV). Jesus was tempted in every way as you have been and yet He did not sin. Ask Him to strengthen you and He will. With every temptation He will make a way of escape if you want it and look for it (1 Corinthians 10:13).

As lying is part of the enemy's warfare, truth is part of the Christian's warfare. You need to be honest in your business affairs, honest in your private life and honest with your words at all times. Jesus said, "I am the way, the truth, and the life . . ." (John 14:6). If we're living as His disciples we will walk in truth.

Jesus, speaking to those who tried to kill Him, said,

> "You are of your father the devil, and you want to do the desires of your father. He was a murderer from the beginning, and does not stand in the truth, because there is no truth in him. Whenever he speaks a lie, he speaks from his own nature; for he is a liar, and the father of lies."
>
> John 8:44, NAS

Those are potent words. Jude (verse 9) says even Michael the archangel did not bring "reviling accusation" against the enemy—a "reviling accusation" means abusive and insulting language. In our spiritual warfare we are not to do that either, but we are on safe ground to call Satan whatever Jesus and the Scriptures call him—the father of lies, thief, deceiver, wicked or evil one, destroyer, murderer, serpent—because those terms describe him accurately.

If the enemy were allowed to come to an important meeting

and told that he could not have a vote in the final decisions of the group, I imagine he might say that all he wants is a voice in the proceedings. He knows that those who are foolish enough to listen to him will give him all the votes he needs! We must be careful not to give the enemy a hearing.

The Breastplate of Righteousness

Righteousness is obviously important since it's mentioned 305 times in the Bible—but what does it mean? God's righteousness is totally different from human self-righteousness. When you accepted Jesus you gave Him your dirty old rags, including your self-righteousness, and He gave you a spotless robe of *His* righteousness. You didn't earn it; it was a free gift of grace (Isaiah 64:6; 61:10; Romans 3:21–26).

What is righteousness? It isn't a list of do's and don't's a mile long. It means doing things in just the right way, the way Jesus would do them. Some years ago Dennis and I ordered storm windows. The salesman showed us samples of how perfectly these windows would be made and installed. When the workman came to put in the windows, however, he didn't have the right tools, and when Dennis inspected the work at the end of the day he found the man had not done a good job at all. He had not mitered corners, but roughly butted boards together, his excuse being that his saw was broken! He had even used a section of wood that was clearly rotten.

Understandably, Dennis was not happy with the work. But instead of calling up the young man's boss and possibly getting him fired, he simply told him he could not accept the job, and that he'd have to do it over. The next day Dennis took many hours to show the young man how he wanted the job done, lent him his own electric saw and showed him how to miter the corners properly. You see, Dennis wanted the work done righteously—that is, correctly; but I think he was also righteous in the way he dealt with the young workman. I believe that's how Jesus would have us handle things.

You need to take God's breastplate and put it on over your heart (the center of your soul, including your motivational life or subconscious mind) to protect this vital area. The question "What would Jesus do?" and, more specifically, "What would Jesus have me do?" should be written at the center of your breastplate. Remind yourself of these questions, and practice the presence of Jesus daily.

Christians can't get away with living unrighteously. When we try it, the Holy Spirit within us is grieved, our consciences bother us and life seems hollow. Our renewed spirits know something is wrong and try to warn us by letting us get depressed and miserable. The answer is to confess our sins and be cleansed, and perhaps, too, seek and receive prayer for inner wholeness.

The word *breastplate,* from the Greek *thorax,* refers to an armored leather doublet that covered the upper body and perhaps extended down to the thighs. I am happy to point out that it protected both front and back! You don't have to have an uncomfortable feeling about your back being exposed; it is protected, too.[5] Isaiah says, "The Lord will go before you, and the God of Israel will be your rear guard" (52:12). In this battle your General goes before you to lead you, and He also comes behind you to protect you. He is your omnipresent Lord.

Shoes of the Gospel of Peace

"How beautiful upon the mountains are the feet of him who brings good news, who proclaims peace, who brings glad tidings of good things, who proclaims salvation, who says to Zion, 'Your

God reigns!' '' (Isaiah 52:7). The message we bring is that of knowing the peace of God; it's not negative but positive. It's a message of peace, but not the kind of peace in which truth must be compromised. We're to lead people out of turmoil and confusion into the shelter of God's peace. Once they've experienced God's peace they will know the difference. "The kingdom of God is . . . righteousness, and peace, and joy in the Holy Ghost" (Romans 14:17, KJV).

Centuries ago when Roman soldiers engaged the enemy in hand-to-hand combat, shoes not only were a protection but also helped give balance. When we lose God's peace we know we're off-balance.

Paul in Romans 10:15 says, "And how shall they preach unless they are sent? As it is written: 'How beautiful are the feet of those who preach the gospel of peace, who bring glad tidings of good things!' '' In the natural, feet are not very attractive things, are they? But God says our feet are not just pretty; they're *beautiful!* Your feet are beautiful whether you think so or not! Jesus showed His love for those who would carry the Good News when He washed the disciples' feet. Our Head, the Lord Jesus Christ, doesn't say to us, His feet, "I have no need of you" (1 Corinthians 12:21).

You are needed, you are called, you are sent by God to bring others His "peace that passes understanding." Jesus needs the feet of Zion, His Church.

The Shield of Faith

The substance of the Christian's shield is made of faith—faith in God and His trustworthiness. If you don't trust a person it blocks your friendship. To trust a person means you have faith in him. God is one hundred percent trustworthy; He is one hundred percent faithful (Lamentations 3:22–23; Isaiah 11:5).

The Greek says, "In all [*en pasin*], take the shield of faith." The King James Version says, "Above all, taking the shield of faith." The Basic English Translation says, "Most of all, using faith as a cover." Above *all* other things God wants you to trust Him, to have faith in Him. If you don't have faith in God you won't believe in any of the armor, receive it or make use of it. Can you imagine what it would be like to go into battle well-armed, but without any confidence in your commander-in-chief? Your salvation is through faith in a Person—Jesus Christ (Ephesians 2:8).

The late Rev. Edward Winkley, an Anglican minister, had an acrostic for the letters in the word faith that I appreciate:

Forsaking
All [others]
I
Take
Him

That's what you did when you accepted Jesus—you took up the shield of faith. Forsaking all other lords in your life, you chose Jesus Christ as your one and only Lord (Hebrews 12:2; 13:5).

Roman soldiers had two different kinds of shields but the one referred to in Ephesians 6 is oblong, about four feet tall and a little over two feet wide. The Greek word for this shield is derived from the word meaning "door" or "gate." It was similar in shape to a curved door. A soldier on the front lines could plant the shield on the ground and conceal himself behind it.

Paul in Ephesians says the shield of faith will protect us from all the fiery darts of the enemy (6:16), but in order to have this protection we must carry the shield with us, and get behind it when the battle is raging.

The Helmet of Salvation

The Greek word for salvation used here in Ephesians is *soteria,* of which the first meaning in the lexicon is "preservation in danger, deliverance from pending death." Through Christ, then, you wear a helmet of preservation, a helmet of deliverance!

Your salvation is in three dimensions: past, present and future. If you have received Jesus, your spirit has been saved; your soul has been saved and is being saved; your body is being saved and will be saved.

Salvation is solid like a helmet and is for your total person. Through it you understand your yesterdays, where you are now and where you are going. Paul says, "But let us who are of the day be sober [not drunk; head clear for clear thinking], putting on the breastplate of faith and love, and as a helmet the hope of salvation" (1 Thessalonians 5:8). We have the joy of our salvation and preservation right now, although we also look for its completion at the resurrection of our bodies.

The helmet of salvation is given to you to protect your mind. Your mind is a treasure. It is composed of your thinking and reasoning power, your willpower and your emotions. The term *mind,* therefore, can be used interchangeably with *soul.* Your mind is not your brain, although your physical brain is part of the equipment or machinery of your mind and soul.

When you were born into God's family you were given the "mind of Christ" (1 Corinthians 2:16). That is to say, you have potentially the reasoning power, the will and the emotions of Jesus Christ. But you must allow His mind to be in you. Philippians 2:5 says, "Let this mind be in you which was also in Christ Jesus." You need to spend time allowing God to give you His thoughts, His will and His emotions—especially in relating to others and helping them. Putting others down or being critical of them is not allowing the mind of Christ to be manifest through you. Loving people and looking for the best in them makes you a healing influence. The helmet of salvation keeps you living in whole thinking, not in sick thinking. As a helmet protects, so must you protect your thinking from influences that make you unloving. Remember, too, that you tend to become like those you spend the most time with.

Your subconscious mind is like a computer with good and bad information and memories stored in it, and emotions connected to those memories. What you meditate on, as well as what you repress, gets stored deeply within your mind. Your subconscious is a very important part of you and you should guard what goes into it. "Keep your heart with all diligence, for out of it spring the issues of life" (Proverbs 4:23). It's true the term *subconscious* is not found in the Bible, but the words *heart, reins, reins of the heart* and *innermost parts* are found there, and they speak of this subconscious part of your soul. Proverbs 18:8 says, "The words of a talebearer are as wounds, and they go down into the innermost parts of the belly" (KJV). Psalm 26:2 says, "Examine me, O Lord, and prove me; try my reins and my heart" (KJV), and Psalm 16:7 says, "My reins also instruct me in the night seasons" (KJV). This is why it's important to share your hurts and pray them "out," so they won't be stored so deeply that they control you unwittingly.

The helmet of salvation also helps you keep your thinking straight. Isaiah 26:3 says, "You will keep him in perfect peace, whose mind is stayed on You, because he trusts in You." Numerous thoughts try to bombard your mind each day and lure you away from the goals God is calling you to. You have the power to resist them and cast them down, as 2 Corinthians 10:4–5 tells you. Though your spirit was made new, your thought life needs continually to be renewed and centered in what happened at your salvation.

The Sword of the Spirit, Which Is the Word of God

The Roman soldier could not fight without his sword. Most other equipment was defensive: the helmet to protect the head, the breastplate for the heart and body, and so forth. The sword could be used defensively, too, but its main purpose was for offense.[6]

How do we use this weapon—this sword, which is the Word of God? Let's look at the meaning of *the Word of God*.

Many Christians are in the habit of using "the Word" mainly to mean the Bible, even though the Bible normally refers to itself as "the Scriptures." Almost always when the Bible speaks of "the Word" it is talking about Jesus Christ Himself, or about something God has said. *The Word*, in this sense, means everything God has revealed to us about Himself through and in His Son, who is Himself therefore the Word, the living Word, the Logos. This is not referring to a particular spoken or written word, but to the whole Truth of God. *Logos* means "Word," as when you say, "What's the word on that?", which means, "Tell me all about it."

The "sword of the Spirit" Paul is talking about in Ephesians, however, is not referring to the Scriptures as a whole or to the Person of Jesus but to an appropriate word or passage from the Scriptures inspired by the Lord for a specific situation. In the

Greek this is called a *rhema,* and this is the term Paul uses in Ephesians 6:17.

The great spiritual example of this, of course, is found in Jesus' temptation in the wilderness. Jesus was clothed with the whole armor of God but He used the sword of Scripture to defeat Satan in battle.

That is, Jesus used *rhemata*—phrases from the Scriptures that God had spoken and that Jesus was inspired by the Spirit to use again in this particular battle. When Satan tempted Him in the wilderness, Jesus Christ, who is personally the Word— God made flesh—took the literal Scriptures from Deuteronomy and used them as living, sword-like words spoken to defeat the enemy. Thus we see "the Word" portrayed in all three dimensions: Jesus, the Word made flesh; the written words of Scripture; and the written Word when it becomes a living word from God.

God's Word is described in the Bible as a two-edged sword. Actually the Greek word we translate "two-edged" means "two-mouthed." This figure of speech is used in Revelation 1:16 in which the Son of Man is portrayed with a two-edged sword coming out of His mouth. Most of the commentators emphasize that this means it was an especially sharp sword and that may be true, because Hebrews 4:12 says, "For the word of God is quick, and powerful, and sharper than any two edged sword, piercing even to the dividing asunder of soul and spirit . . ." (Hebrews 4:12, KJV). God's Word can certainly distinguish between that which is from our reborn spirits, and that which is from our partially renewed souls.[7]

The two edges could be interpreted in several other ways: There is the distinction between Jesus Himself, the living Word (Hebrews 4:12) who speaks to us by His Spirit in our spirits, and then the holy Scriptures as the written Word. The Bible itself cannot save you; it can never replace a living, personal relationship with Jesus. But it will show you the way to Him and tell you about Him so that you can receive Him. We need both the living Word and the written Word, since you and I in this confusing world don't always hear from God clearly.

Another dimension of this is to say that there is both a literal and spiritual meaning of Scripture. If you look only at the literal meaning, you can have an interesting historical study, but receive little or no spiritual food, direction or inspiration. If you read only for spiritual refreshment, on the other hand, learning nothing of the foundational and historical background of Scripture, you may end up with some strange concepts.

There's no reason for us not to have a working knowledge of the Scriptures. There are good books and good teachers who can help us, if we will seek them out by the guidance of the Spirit, but most of all reading the Bible daily will keep us discerning so that we can tell whether or not things we hear or read have the "flavor" of Jesus and His love. Someone said the Bible is like a road map; it needs to be consulted every day of the journey!

There's no question, no matter what our interpretations may be, that we need this sword of the Spirit at all times for our safety along the road of life.

Praying Always in the Spirit

Praying in the Spirit in the past was not usually classed as a part of the armor simply because it wasn't understood. In this day, with the renewed understanding of the working of the Holy Spirit, millions of people have found it to be so. This seventh piece of the armor is most often overlooked because it's invisible: You can't make a picture of it as clothing or equipment, because this is not what the soldier wears but what comes out of his mouth.

It can function as a sword, though. Songs of deliverance and praise are potent weapons. Look at these verses: "Let the saints be joyful in glory; let them sing aloud on their beds. Let the high praises of God be in their mouth, and a two-edged sword in their hand" (Psalm 149:5–6). Have you ever sung praises to God while in bed? If you're not the morning type, perhaps you can try singing at night! God's way of fighting battles is certainly different from ours. High praises of God speak of praising God in the highest way—"in the Spirit." (For the best Scripture explanation of "praying in the Spirit" see 1 Corinthians 14:13–19.)

I'll never forget the time I heard singing in the Spirit at a meeting in Nacogdoches, Texas, in 1961. As people began to sing in the Spirit, the Holy Spirit moved so strongly that a man on the front row fell to his knees crying out to God, and a young man in the back row was immediately released in the Spirit and began praising God in new freedom. It was so exciting! All praise is like armor, and praise in the Spirit is even more powerful— yes, even like a sword.

In chapter 4 we looked at the Old Testament example of King Jehoshaphat and how he handled things when several armies came to dethrone him (2 Chronicles 20:1–30). Remember how Jehoshaphat did something army generals just don't do? He appointed singers to go before his army to praise God. As they praised the Lord and sang, the enemy's armies wiped each other out! Today, *you* can see victories won through your high praises to God. Churches, too, can see battles won through the power of supernatural praise and song.

Don't forget you need the constant filling and overflowing of God's Spirit so you'll know what Jesus would have you do and say.[8] Ephesians 5:18–19 says, "And be not drunk with wine, wherein is excess; but be filled with the Spirit; speaking to yourselves in psalms and hymns and spiritual songs, singing and making melody in your heart to the Lord" (KJV). In the literal Greek, verse 18 would be translated something like, "*Be being* filled with the Spirit." That is, keep on being filled with God's Spirit day by day, hour by hour, moment by moment. *Once is not enough.* This is the way to victory for yourself and others.

The Armor Is Summed Up in Jesus

Some years ago as I prepared to write an article and traced these seven pieces of armor through the Scriptures, I realized that Jesus Himself *is* all of these things:

He is the *Belt of Truth* encircling us: "Jesus said to him, 'I am the way, the truth, and the life' " (John 14:6).

He is our *Breastplate:* "The Lord our righteousness" (Jeremiah 33:16; 23:6; Malachi 4:2).

He is the *Gospel of Peace:* "For He Himself is our peace" (Ephesians 2:14) and He leads our feet on the pathway to bring this good news to others.

He is our *Shield of Faith:* "Looking unto Jesus, the author and finisher of our faith" (Hebrews 12:2). One friend put it this way: "Faith is the Person of Christ living in and through my spirit. What He gives me is Himself—not just a conviction that could be called faith." In Genesis 15:1 the Lord says, "I am your shield, your exceedingly great reward."

He is our *Helmet of Salvation:* "The Lord is my light and my salvation" (Psalm 27:1). As the prophet Simeon held the Baby Jesus he said, "Lord, . . . my eyes have seen Your salvation" (Luke 2:29–30).

He is the *Sword of the Spirit,* the Word of God: "In the beginning was the Word, and the Word was with God, and the Word was God" (John 1:1). Speaking of this further, the writer of Hebrews said, "For the word of God [Jesus] is living and powerful, and sharper than any two-edged sword" (Hebrews 4:12; see also verses 13–16, which show the Word first and foremost to be Jesus Christ Himself).

He is our *Praise:* Jeremiah said to God, "You are my praise" (17:14). John the Baptist said of Jesus, "He will baptize you with the Holy Spirit and fire" (Matthew 3:11). Jesus gives us prayer in the Spirit; He is the Baptizer.

Jesus is the embodiment of all the weapons of spiritual warfare so we must *put on Jesus Christ.* We did this when we received Jesus, and it was testified to by baptism with water, as Galatians 3:27 reminds us. But Romans 13:14 tells us as baptized believers to do it again as a protection from temptation: "Put on the Lord Jesus Christ, and make no provision for the flesh, to fulfill its lusts." What greater protection can there be?

One family of adults and children in Charlotte, North Carolina, prays in a particular way each day. They begin by reading Scripture and conclude by putting on the whole armor of God verbally and praying together in the Spirit. What a great way to start the day!

Whether you do it alone or with your family, remember to "keep yourself" (1 John 5:18) by putting on the entire armor of God daily; do it just as naturally as you put your clothes on daily. Let it become a good habit in your life along with the habit of praying the Lord's Prayer.

And as you do, remember this privilege was purchased by the blood Jesus shed.

It is vitally important to claim and proclaim verbally the protection of the blood of Jesus over your own spirit, soul and body, over your family and your home, and over any means of transportation for that day.

I know you'll find this helpful to use in conjunction with praying this concluding part of Jesus' prayer, and these activities will keep you ready for anything God should want you to do to further His Kingdom.

You Have Power Over Evil

You may think, *I've put the armor on, but now do I have power to do anything?* Jesus said to the seventy disciples, "Behold, I give you the authority to trample on serpents and scorpions, and over all the power of the enemy, and nothing shall by any means hurt you" (Luke 10:19). He meant these words for you as well as for the seventy. "Serpents and scorpions" in Scripture refers to Satan and his demonic workers.

There is no need to be afraid; just know that you have power over *all* the power of the enemy through Jesus' blood and in His name. Memorize this verse for your arsenal. This is not a pretend war, but one in which you have been involved from the moment you accepted Jesus and particularly after your empowering with the Holy Spirit. You're no match for Satan on your own! *But you are not on your own.* You have Christ Jesus in you, the One in whose name every evil spirit must bow.

Some of the things God needs to deliver you and me from, all too often, are our own evil thinking and wrong ways of speaking and acting. Sometimes we can be our own worst enemies. In the previous chapter we saw that we could be our own "tempters" at times. But we need also to be delivered from the evil intentions of others against us.

If you have unhealed wounds from the mistreatments of others,

153

God wants to and can heal you. Jesus wept with you when you wept and has a plan for your restoration. He couldn't stop the evil done against you and others without taking away their free will—making them robots. God could, of course, wipe out the entire human race, but then He'd destroy both the evil and the good. That's why Jesus says the wheat and the weeds will have to grow together until the battle between good and evil has ended at harvest time, at the end of this age (Matthew 13:29, 37). Some of those who are now doing evil may repent and become God's choice servants. Look at Mary Magdalene, for instance, who had seven demons cast out of her; or Saul who was hunting down Christians. Or look at you and me and what God has done to change our lives through His grace.

Adults, and young people, too, who know their authority in Christ have with a word been able to stop demonized people who were coming at them to do them harm. Missionary Henry B. Garlock in his book, *Before We Kill and Eat You,* tells how he was about to be killed by cannibals when the Holy Spirit supernaturally gave him the ability to speak to them in their own tribal language. Not only was his life saved by what the Holy Spirit spoke through him, but Kelso, the man he was attempting to rescue, was saved from a horrible death and the whole village came to Christ.[9] That's effective evangelization for sure!

This is a good example of why Jesus has us ask the Father to deliver us from evil and also tells *us* to cast out the evil (Mark 16:17). Both are obviously necessary. Remember that you aren't doing this on your own and you can trust that God is doing what He promised. But you must do your part; you must walk in the authority God has given you through the name of Jesus and learn to wield the sword of the Spirit as Jesus did.

A good sword to use against the evil intentions of others against you is found in Isaiah 54:17:

> No weapon that is formed against you shall prosper, and every tongue that shall rise against you in judgment you shall show to be in the wrong. This [peace, righteousness, security, triumph over opposition] is the heritage of the servants of the Lord [those in whom the ideal Servant of the Lord is reproduced]. This is the righteousness or the vindication which they obtain from Me—this is that which I impart to them as their justification—says the Lord.
>
> AMPLIFIED

When you were a small child it was almost physically impossible for you to get away from mistreatment; but now God cannot only heal you from those hurts, as we learned earlier, but protect you from new hurts as you are in fellowship with Him and know how to do spiritual warfare when it is needed. God wants only good things for His children, but when your life is being challenged by evil you have a choice to make and mustn't sit by passively and do nothing. God has equipped you with His armor and His power.

You can also be delivered from the enemy by doing the things he hates, like loving unconditionally, repenting, forgiving everyone, praying in the Spirit, praying with your understanding, applying yourself to studying the Gospels—which really contain Jesus' last will and testament!—going on to the Acts of the Apostles, the epistles, Psalms, Proverbs and the rest of the Bible. Further important things are setting captives free by soul (inner) healing prayer, deliverance and spiritual warfare, intercessory prayers, praise and worship, receiving the Lord's Supper, to name some basics.

Now, in review, here are the steps for inner wholeness or healing found in the Lord's Prayer, as set forth in this book:

Our Father:

1. Receive the unconditional love of God: Father, Son and Holy Spirit—especially the healing of your father relationship through your heavenly Father.

In heaven. Holy is Your name:

2. Practice the omnipresence of a holy God—past, present and future; know that God's love has always been with you and experience it now.

Your Kingdom come:

3. His Kingdom has been established in your spirit, making all other healing possible.

Your will be done, on earth as in heaven:

4. Yield your will to God for healing and for His Lordship.

Give us today our daily bread:

5. Take time to rest in the Lord, and even though you make plans for the future, adopt the attitude of taking one day at a time.

And forgive us our sins:

6. Ask God's forgiveness for sins you were unaware of until you were healed inside; this is especially true for hurts that were repressed in your subconscious. Your known sins are dealt with

by repentance, confession and assurance of God's forgiveness—what many would term "absolution."

As we forgive those who sin against us:

7. Forgive others their sins against you with your will and, when needed, spend more time in Jesus' healing presence for deeper healing, enabling you to forgive with your emotions.

Lead us not into temptation:

8. Pray for healing weak areas of vulnerability to sin where you are or have been most easily tempted.

But deliver us from evil:

9. Pray for healing the effects of evil done to you, especially in childhood and young adult years.

Receive deliverance prayer for demonic depression, oppression or temporary invasion of the soul through gross sins. (As with Russell's experience, seek help from loving, experienced Christians who understand soul healing as well as deliverance prayer.)

For Yours is the Kingdom, and the power, and the glory forever:

10. Praise is not only refreshing communication with God—Father, Son and Holy Spirit—but also brings with it a sword of protection, as was mentioned earlier. *Praise gets our thoughts back on God,* the One who is the central focus of our lives. Even as the Lord's Prayer ends in praise, so we find this an important part of concluding our prayers for inner wholeness. (We'll be looking at the doxology of praise in the next chapter.)

The Interpreter's Bible says, "We pray, 'Deliver us from sickness, fear, poverty, unpopularity'; but cannot understand why we should pray, *Deliver us from evil*. The wrong in the world is not merely economic or psychological maladjustment, though these factors may be present: it is wickedness. So this prayer has deep meaning. It admits our weakness, pleads for hatred of evil, and therefore breathes our love for God."[10]

There's protection in praying these words in faith: *Deliver us from evil and from the evil one*. I usually quote a personalized version of Jesus' promise in Luke 10:19 at this point: "I have been given power over all the power of the enemy, and nothing shall by any means hurt me!" This part of the Lord's Prayer reminds us of the dangers on a planet that has strayed from God, but also that we have power to do something about it. And who knows? Maybe God will even use it to bring angels to our aid.

Though I can't attempt to give all the reasons, I know He said, "Do it."

Prayer

"But deliver us from evil . . ."

Dear Father, whatever has happened in my life that was obviously evil did not come from You, my loving God. Teach me how to live in Your protection. Thank You that I can trust You, Your Son and the Spirit *totally*. Abba [Daddy], You are a good Parent wanting only the best for me, Your child. As Your Son, Jesus Christ, taught me, I pray, "Deliver me from evil and from the evil one" this day and every day, and deliver my family, too.

Deliver me from the evil intentions of others against me; because I'm walking in right relationship with You and others I can claim Your word spoken through Isaiah: No weapon formed against me shall prosper, and those who speak evil against me will be exposed, for this is my heritage in You, dear Lord.

Deliver me from the influence of the evil one. Help me walk close to Your Son, so I'll be safe from demonic influence in the world. Teach me to use my rightful authority to resist evil and set captives free. Thank You that I have "authority over all the power of the enemy and *nothing* shall by any means hurt me." I claim Your protection, and the protection of the blood of Jesus, over my loved ones and myself, also my pet(s), belongings and work.

And deliver me from any concealed evil in my own thinking, speaking, acting. Set me free from anything that is not of You and Your Kingdom. I'm glad someone realized that *evil,* turned around, spells *live.* Where still needed, convert my soul and turn it around so that I may truly live life to the full.

All these things I pray in the name of Jesus Christ, Your Son, and through His blood given for me.

[*Take time here to visualize prayerfully putting on the whole armor of God.*]

Pause and reflect.

13
The Doxology of the Lord's Prayer

The earliest manuscripts of the New Testament do not have the familiar ending to the Lord's Prayer, "For Yours is the kingdom and the power and the glory forever. Amen." For this reason most scholars do not believe Jesus Himself put these words of praise at the end of the prayer, but that they were added later.

If so, whoever added them was certainly led by the Spirit of God, obviously feeling that the Lord's Prayer should culminate in praise. I'm glad, too, that the Holy Spirit saw to it that it was in the manuscripts used by the 47 scholars who translated the King James Version, and that many other translators have followed suit.[1] Most churches in the Protestant tradition use it, and because this closing doxology is so revered and such a tool of praise, I have included it, too. I love its victorious words, which bring Jesus' prayer to a conclusion, as well as remind us of the importance of praise to God in our prayer lives.

Dr. George Buttrick, editor of *The Interpreter's Bible*, says, "The phrase was almost certainly not in the original prayer. . . . But we may be glad for the addition; it is a final peal of trumpets. Christ prompted this doxology. Why should a small and persecuted church add such a climax of praise to a prayer taught them by One from Galilee? . . . The doxology of the Lord's Prayer is the church's praise for his risen power. His prayer became a nobler temple: God's redeeming presence. Therefore the early church said, For thine is the kingdom. . . ."[2]

For Yours Is the Kingdom

The first phrase of this doxology reminds us that the Kingdom is His and not ours. Shortly after Jesus gave the prayer He said, "Seek first the kingdom of God and His righteousness" (Matthew 6:33). Christians need to be more aware that personal "kingdom-building" is a real temptation and has caused the downfall of many a good work. The first disciples themselves had a hard time avoiding it. After being with Jesus for a while, they came to Him asking, "Who then is greatest in the kingdom of heaven?" (Matthew 18:1). Jesus called a little child over to Him and used their own question to teach them about being childlike: "Therefore whoever humbles himself as this little child is the greatest in the kingdom of heaven" (Matthew 18:4).

Just before the crucifixion, James and John came to ask if they might sit on the right and left of His throne when He came into His Kingdom. Jesus explained that that decision was up to His Father (Mark 10:35–41). At the Last Supper the disciples were still arguing over which one was going to be the greatest (Luke 22:24–30)! Even after the resurrection and before the ascension they asked Jesus if He was now going to restore the Kingdom to Israel (Acts 1:6), ostensibly so they could hold high office in it! (Sound familiar?) Jesus replied, "It is not for you to know times or seasons which the Father has put in His own authority." He then pointed them to what would help them most: "But you shall receive power when the Holy Spirit has come upon you" (Acts 1:7–8). After this empowerment, their immediate job would not be to sit down in the Kingdom, but to spread the Kingdom to the world.

Human kingdom-building in Christian organizations, denominations, movements within the Church, will all be tested by the Lord. It's great to see good works grow, but the bigger they get the more their leaders can be faced with temptations to pride and power.

I like a song that Conrad, my son by marriage, wrote, which says, "Kings may come and kings may go . . . Jesus is forever."[3] How true! Kingdoms may come and kingdoms may go, but Jesus' Kingdom is forever. You and I are not here to build earthly kingdoms, which will only pass away, but rather to build His, which is holy and eternal.

Which kingdom will you build? God's Kingdom? Your kingdom or another human kingdom? Or, knowingly or unknowingly, the usurper's kingdom? As the heavenly messengers told the young woman who had had the critical car wreck in chapter 4, your love for God will show by what you do with your life and whom you serve.

And the Power

Of power, George Buttrick says, "What kind of power? Power in what motive? Power for what end? Lord Acton said, 'Power tends to corrupt, and absolute power corrupts absolutely.' He meant man's pride in power. What of the power that surrenders power in love? This doxology is the praise of the early church in the contemplation of God's power through Calvary and Easter. . . . If we do not worship God in constant doxology, we shall end in a grotesque and ruinous self-worship."[4]

Just before Jesus went to take His place at His Father's side He told His friends, "All power has been given Me in heaven and on the earth!" (Matthew 28:18, literal Greek). We don't know the actual Aramaic Jesus used, but the Greek here is *exousia,* which means authority.[5] Jesus has ultimate authority over everything, including the evil one and his work.

When the originator of this doxology said, "Thine is the power," however, he used another Greek word for power, *dunamis,* the one from which we get the word *dynamite.* Jesus demonstrated this kind of power when He walked on water, healed the sick, raised the dead.

Imagine a policeman directing traffic. He has authority *(exousia)* to make you stop, but he does not have power *(dunamis)* to stop your car forcibly by pushing on the front bumper!

While the war between God's light and Satan's darkness is still going on in this world, the Lord limits His own *dunamis,* His dynamite, because although it could wipe out all the bad things in the world, it would also destroy many people who might yet come to know God. This is what "the age of grace" means— God limiting His power instead of exercising it directly, thus by His love giving the world a chance to change. He works today by making His power and love available through His people by the Holy Spirit.

His *dunamis* begins to be released through you when you receive Jesus and the power of the Holy Spirit. God can then work through you to heal the sick, set captives free, help the brokenhearted, feed the hungry and in every way possible draw people to Him.

A college student said to a friend of mine, "It's hard to believe there is a God, because really bad things happened to me when I was a child, and an all-powerful God would have stopped them.'' She needed someone to explain to her the reason for the age of grace.

Jesus exercised great power when He was on earth, but His *dunamis* in heaven and earth won't be fully released until the end of this age. In the book of Revelation both *exousia* and *dunamis* are used to describe God's Kingdom coming in its fullness: ''Now have come the salvation and the power [*dunamis*] and the kingdom of our God, and the authority [*exousia*] of his Christ'' (Revelation 12:10, NIV). He's already reigning in His people, but it's a day to look forward to when the Kingdom fully comes on this earth.

Because you are in Christ, through God's *exousia* you can say ''Stop'' to the enemy, and he must obey you; and by God's *dunamis* Jesus can work through you to destroy the works of the enemy by which he harasses and tries to destroy the people of God. You may function both in God's power and in His authority; in fact, *He is counting on you to do so*. All this is for your joy, and for God's glory. As you do, you can say, ''Dear God, Yours is the power. Thanks for letting it flow through me!'' The power and authority of God are available to His people because we are already in the Kingdom.

Jesus said we would do greater things than even He had done (John 14:12). He made the way but we must learn to walk in it; this takes practice and effort, as anything worth accomplishing does.

And the Glory For Ever and Ever

Most of His time on earth Jesus spent as an everyday person doing everyday things, such as working in the family carpentry shop. Even after His ministry began, only at certain times did He let His true identity show.

On the Mount of Transfiguration His glory was seen briefly by three of the disciples: "His face shone like the sun, and his clothes became as white as the light" (Matthew 17:2, NIV). When the soldiers came to arrest Him, they asked which one was Jesus of Nazareth, and He answered, "I AM." As He said these words the soldiers all "went backward, and fell to the ground," as bowling pins do when the ball strikes them (John 18:6, KJV).

The night before His crucifixion He prayed, "And now, O Father, glorify Me together with Yourself, with the glory which I had with You before the world was" (John 17:5). As Jesus died, there was a tremendous earthquake, the veil of the Temple was torn in two; and Matthew tells us that tombs broke open and "many holy people" who had died were brought back to earthly life, just as Lazarus had been in John 11 (Matthew 27:52, NIV).

Yet the greatest manifestation of Jesus' glory was seen when He rose from the dead in His resurrection body. The radiation from His body at that moment was so powerful many believe it imprinted a three-dimensional picture of itself on His burial clothes.

The manifestation of Christ's divinity is glory! Handel's great "Hallelujah Chorus" ends with, "The kingdom of this world is become the Kingdom of our Lord and of His Christ . . . and He shall reign for ever and ever. . . . King of Kings and Lord of Lords, and He shall reign . . . for ever and ever. . . . Hallelujah!" Everyone stands during this chorus to give glory and honor to God. What a thrill it was to be part of a five thousand-voice choir at a Billy Graham outdoor crusade in Los Angeles in 1964. The air seemed to continue to ring and echo back to us even after we had stopped singing. To my mind it was as if an angel choir continued to sing, and perhaps it did, for many had come into the Kingdom that night.

Kingdom living may sometimes seem a long way in the future. True, its fullness will not take place till then, but when Jesus comes to live in you by the Holy Spirit, His Kingdom is set up in you now. It's *His* Kingdom, but He has chosen to share it with you. He said to His Father, "And the glory which You gave Me *I have given them,* that they may be one just as We are one" (John 17:22). He has given you a share in the same glory His Father gave Him! That's awesome! His power and authority and glory are with and in you right now. You're supposed to be living in the Kingdom while on earth, as a king or queen under direction of the King of kings. He said, "All authority has been given to Me." Then He said, "Go therefore . . . ," indicating that you and I are to go in that same authority (Matthew 28:18–19).

It's His Kingdom, His power and His glory—yet He has chosen to share it with you! You are important to God. If you will allow Him, He will use you to make a real difference in His world, and you will have the joy of helping Him usher in His Kingdom. You will rule and reign with Him, and the time to get ready for it is now. Praying and living the Lord's Prayer can be part of your readiness program.

Amen

Amen means "truly." It is the word Jesus used that our English Bible also translates as "verily" or "most assuredly" or "truly" or "I tell you the truth." *The Interpreter's Bible* again says it well: "It is man's resolve: 'So let it be!' It is, more deeply, trust and assurance that God can bring great things to pass: 'So let it be!' By right instinct the church added a doxology and an amen to the Lord's Prayer."[6]

I say "Amen" to that!

The Lord's Prayer ends with our amen: "Let it be so, Lord!" But we can confidently know that God the Father adds His own amen to His Son's great prayer: "It *shall* be so!" So when you pray "Amen" at the conclusion of the Lord's Prayer, remember you can say, "It shall be so," because God has "told you the truth"; "truly" and "most assuredly" He has!

Prayer

"For Yours is the Kingdom,

Dear Father, forgive me when I've forgotten that it's Your Kingdom I'm building, and not my own or anyone else's. All other kingdoms will pass away, but Yours is forever! I am committed to building Your Kingdom alone, this day and every day. May Your Kingdom of love flow through me today.

"and the power,

Thank You for sharing Your power, both Your authority and Your dynamic power, with me, by Your incoming and outflowing experiences in my life. I know the flow is always within me when it's needed; help me learn not to block it. Increase my capacity to receive Your power.

"and the glory forever.

Thank You for sharing Your glory with the Church of which I am a part. Let Your glory be seen in and upon me when it will benefit Your Kingdom. I am available to You, Lord God. Thank You for the awesome privileges You give Your children who love You.

I praise Your Son, Jesus, for sharing His authority, power and glory with me and for the Holy Spirit's part in this. I will never take these, Your gifts, lightly. Show me how to be a credit to Your name and His name. If I've received any trophies, I count it joy to lay them at Your feet at the close of each day, and one day to lay them before Your throne in heaven above (Revelation 4:10–11).

"To him who sits on the throne and to the Lamb be praise and honor and glory and power, for ever and ever! . . . Amen" (Revelation 5:13–14, NIV).

"Amen.

I am assured by God that this is the truth. Thank You, God, that it is done!

"In Jesus' name."

[I believe those who wish to acknowledge that they pray in Jesus' name should feel free to do so. We know He told us that we were to pray petitionary prayers to our Father in the name of Jesus (John 16:23–24, 26). Though Jesus didn't mention for us to do this at the end of the Lord's Prayer, He undoubtedly thought we'd understand that you do something "in a person's name" when you do it through his authority. Since Jesus gave you the prayer, you're doing it in His name whether or not you actually say it at the end. I'm sure our Lord would be happy for you to choose to conclude His prayer "in Jesus' name," as I sometimes do.]

Pause, reflect and praise

14
Intercessory Prayer

When you have completed praying the Lord's Prayer reflectively and putting on God's armor, you are ready for anything and everything! And if you have time following these prayers, or whenever you have five or ten minutes during the day or night, you know that you are cleansed and ready to pray for those who are in need. The prayers of a right-thinking, -speaking and -acting person are productive and powerful (James 5:16). Interceding for your family and others is extremely important.

In chapter 1, I mentioned how to use this book to the maximum, and as you read and pray your way through *Inner Wholeness through the Lord's Prayer* and return to it prayerfully as the Lord directs, you will soon be able to move through the prayer in as little as ten or fifteen minutes, or for as long as you have time to pray. Extra busy people can pray in shifts, perhaps starting while still in bed before the alarm goes off, while riding the bus to work, continuing during coffee break, interceding while swimming laps at lunch or jogging. Those working at home can begin right at the breakfast table after getting the family off to school and work, continue while washing dishes or clothes, while ironing, mending or working in the garden, while taking a walk, waiting for the children following music lessons or baseball, football, cheerleading or band practice. You will really find you have a lot more time to pray than you thought, and, may I add, less time to worry!

Meditate on His Word

Read the New Testament, at least a chapter a day. It will help you to know the mind of God. Here is a listing of some good verses that will help prepare you. If you believe them in childlike faith, great things will happen. Some of the promises have conditions connected with them, which I've italicized.

Jesus is speaking in these first four verses:

> "And whatever you ask in My name, that I will do, that the Father may be glorified in the Son. *If you ask anything in My name,* I will do it."
>
> John 14:13–14

> "Most assuredly, I say to you, *whatever you ask the Father in My name* He will give you."
>
> John 16:23

> "*If you abide in Me,* and *My words abide in you,* you will ask what you desire, and it shall be done for you."
>
> John 15:7

> "Therefore I say to you, whatever things you ask when you pray, *believe that you receive them,* and you will have them."
>
> Mark 11:24

And whatever we ask we receive from Him, *because we keep His commandments* and *do those things that are pleasing in His sight.*

1 John 3:22

The late Rev. Canon Clifton Best said, "I sincerely believe that in all the centuries since our Lord made these promises, there has never been a failure to experience their fulfillment—providing the conditions have been met. . . ."[1]

A keynote Scripture on this subject is in Isaiah in which God is specifically calling for intercessors. Isaiah the prophet looked forward to Jesus Christ, the Messiah, who is Himself the great Intercessor, the Way between God and man, and wrote:

He saw that there was no man, and wondered that there was no intercessor [no one to intervene on behalf of truth and right]; therefore His own arm brought Him victory, and His righteousness [having the Spirit without measure] sustained Him. For the Lord put on righteousness as a breastplate or coat of mail, and salvation for a helmet upon His head. . . ."

Isaiah 59:16–17, AMPLIFIED;
compare Ephesians 6:10–18

Through Jesus you and I can share in this great work of intercession—that is, bridging the gap between man's needs and God's overwhelming love.

Think Deeply About God's Love and Presence

If possible, find a quiet spot to pray. Choose not to think of other things. Recall again the two master keys to inner wholeness: God's unconditional love for you and His omnipresence (Jehovah-Shammah)—the keys told about in chapters 2 and 4.

Reflect (meditate) on this *love,* and how "God loved you so much that He gave His only begotten Son so that you would not perish but have everlasting life" (John 3:16, personalized). Think of the Father's sacrifice, and the Son's sacrifice for you. Consider the fullness of God's love,

> that Christ may dwell in your hearts through faith; that you, being rooted and grounded in love, may be able to comprehend with all the saints what is the width and length and depth and height—to know the love of Christ which passes knowledge; that you may be filled with all the fullness of God.
>
> Ephesians 3:17–19

Reflect (meditate) on God's *presence* with you. He was with you in the past even when you didn't know He was there, and He's close by you right now. Think of the Holy Spirit's work in making "Christ in you" possible. Remember the words spoken by our Lord at the Last Supper: "If anyone loves Me . . . My Father will love him, and We will come to him and make Our home with him" (John 14:23). At that same time He said: "At that day you will know that I am in My Father, and you in Me, and I in you" (John 14:20). Recall to memory the great psalm of God's presence, Psalm 139. Commit verses 1–18 of this psalm to memory so you can reflect on it during your prayers. Again, to quote Canon Best: "I tell you truthfully that one can be as conscious of the Presence of God as he can of the presence of any human being. We are conscious of the presence of humans, by or through our physical senses; but we are conscious of

of God's Presence by our spiritual senses—and these are infinitely keener."[2]

Be an Intercessor

According to Webster's, intercession is "prayer, petition, or
entreaty in favor of another," and an intercessor is a person who
is active in this kind of prayer. This step follows your thoughts
about God's love and presence naturally. Pray with childlike
faith, lift people up to God as He brings them to mind, and say
what He gives you to say.

If you'd like a reminder of those whom you might pray for,
you may find this "Petitionary Hand of Prayer" helpful.[3] Consider your hand. Beginning with your thumb, pray for those
closest to you, your mate, children, relatives. Next is your fore-
finger, which is the strongest. Pray for those in strong positions
in the church and the world: your pastor, the leader of your
country and his staff, others in authority in the nation, the state,
the community in which you live. Next comes your middle finger,
which is the longest, so pray for those who are farthest away from
you physically, people you love who are overseas, friends on the
mission field. Then comes your ring finger, which tends to be the
weakest, and can remind you to pray for those who are ill, for the
poor, for the elderly and for those who are in distress of any kind.
Last is your little finger, one you might tie a string around. This
can remind you to pray for yourself.

Praying for yourself is not by definition intercession, but it is
very important because you are important to God. You know
your situation and needs better than anyone on earth. The greatest
intercessory prayer is by Jesus, recorded in John 17; and at this
agonizing time just before His crucifixion, He began by praying
for Himself, then His disciples, then for the whole Church. There

are times when you, too, will need to pray for yourself first before you can help others.

Give Thanks and Praise

You can thank someone for something he has done for you without necessarily knowing him personally. But to praise someone, you have to know him. So although you should certainly thank God for what He has done for you, because you know Him you can praise Him for who He is, and then you will have confidence to thank Him for who you know He's going to do.

I'm glad that our Lord Jesus twice said that those with a mustard seed amount of faith can still do great things. He said that even with this tiny portion you could say to a mulberry tree, "Be pulled up by the roots and be planted in the sea," and it would obey you (Luke 17:6). And you could say to a mountain, " 'Move from here to there,' and it will move; and nothing will be impossible for you" (Matthew 17:20).

Move a mountain? Yes, Jesus said this is possible by your words, with faith in your heart: "Therefore I say to you, whatever things you ask when you pray, believe that you receive them, and you will have them" (Mark 11:24).

Try to exercise your faith; water that mustard seed so it will grow; believe and give thanks even before you receive. As you are praying, when your heart and soul fill with love, *praise God for His goodness, for His love and kindness*. As you do His glory can fill you and the place where you are praying. How do I know? The book of 2 Chronicles says that

> when they lifted up their voice with the trumpets and cymbals and instruments of music, and praised the Lord, saying, For he is good; for his mercy endureth for ever; that

then the house was filled with a cloud, even the house of the Lord; so that the priests could not stand to minister by reason of the cloud; for the glory of the Lord had filled the house of God.

2 Chronicles 5:13–14, KJV

Don't blame God for the evil going on in the world, or in your own life; rather praise Him, verbally and with singing, for His love and goodness, and you'll see the bad turning to good, for you and for others.

Praying the Lord's Prayer for Someone Else

To enjoy praying the Lord's Prayer for someone else, you could use the guideline that follows. The Lord's Prayer is perfect intercession. You could pray it for a person you're concerned about while you're alone, or you could use it together with a mate or friend, hands joined, interceding aloud, one at a time. This method of intercession through the Lord's Prayer was given me as I researched and wrote about the prayer beginning in 1987 for the booklet we published. I taught it on television around that time and in small inner healing prayer groups. When I shared it at a conference of several hundred women in Stratford, Ontario, in 1989 we saw powerful results as the Holy Spirit guided them to pray for one another. I believe it will be helpful to you also.

Intercessory Lord's Prayer

Abba, Daddy in heaven, I lift up and respect your holy name. I pray Your Kingdom come in [name the person]. Your will be done in *him* [or *her*] as it is in heaven. Give *him* today Your daily bread, physically and spiritually. Forgive *his* sins as *he* forgives those who've sinned against *him*. Heal *his* soul [add "and spirit," if the person is not a Christian], that *he* may be able to forgive others, and forgive *himself*.

Good Shepherd, lead [name] safely away from the temptations of the evil one. Deliver *him* and *his* loved ones from all evil, dear Father. For Yours is the Kingdom and the power and the glory forever. According to Your Word let it be so. In Jesus' name.

(Change pronouns as needed, and add to this basic outline as led.)

Be Still and Listen

So often we look to others, especially to Christian leaders, to hear from God for us, instead of taking time to hear from Him ourselves. We want instant gratification of all kinds, even instant "on tap" words from someone who we believe speaks for God. We would rather talk to one person after another about personal conflicts with "irregular people" in our lives, trying to get advice, but often the last person we go to is God. Well-intentioned though it may be, this kind of advice might not be at all what God wants for us. We must grow more mature in our relationship with God, while at the same time maintaining our childlike quality of faith. One way we can do this is to take time to hear from God ourselves.

After I have prayed the Lord's Prayer, put on the armor of God, and interceded for myself and others, I like to think about God's omnipresence and unconditional love for me as I spend time waiting in silence for God's direction or special touch. I'm not *passive*, but alert, with my whole being centered on Him. I believe this is where you and I can find much healing, guidance and protection for our lives. The businessperson can learn what to say at the board meeting, the doctor the diagnosis he seeks, the pastor what to teach God's people and the sick the way to healing.

Before I enter the "secret place of the Most High" to wait before the Lord, I like to begin by praying a personalized version of 2 Corinthians 10:5:

> I "cast down arguments and every high thing that exalts itself against the knowledge of God, and bring every thought into captivity to the obedience of Christ." I thank You, Father, that I am under the protection of the blood of Your Son, Jesus: spirit, soul and body.
>
> I thank You, Lord God, that Your Word says I "have the mind of Christ," and also that I must "let this mind be in [me] which was also in Christ Jesus" (1 Corinthians 2:16; Philippians 2:5). May His will be my will, may His emotions be my emotions, may His thoughts be my thoughts, may His love be my love.
>
> As young Samuel responded when You called to Him, I also pray those same words: "Speak, Lord, your servant is listening" [see 1 Samuel 3:10].

I usually have a pencil and paper nearby to write down what I feel the Lord is saying. Sometimes I pray softly in the Spirit within or aloud, and then return to waiting. I don't try to make anything happen or try to receive a message from God; it is a time of peace and rest. I am just available to God. He has my full attention. I do "triune listening": spirit, soul and body.

I have enjoyed praying this way especially during the concluding evenings over the past ten years while Dennis is teaching at the last service during healing seminars; I find a quiet place, usually the pastor's office, and I pray for Dennis and the congregation. God often impresses me with specific needs of the people present, which are later confirmed. It's always amazing to me how simply God speaks when you remain childlike and open to Him.

When I need special direction for my life, I take this extra time to wait in the quiet with God, and sometimes I fast. In this way I expect to receive what God has told me to pray for. Sometimes He speaks later on when I'm not even expecting it—even in a dream. It may be hard to add this step to your prayer life, but do it as you are led. You will be rewarded. You are praying "to the max."

A Closing Word

Scholars over the years have studied and dissected the Lord's Prayer trying to understand its power and trying to find out if Jesus actually wrote it in its entirety or gave it from a compilation of Hebrew petitions He'd learned from others.

Dr. James Hastings has this to say in response to this question. "(1) Its symmetry and progressive development of thought, and (2) its inexhaustible adaptability, are characteristics which do not harmonize well with the hypothesis that it is a compilation. . . . Let us examine these characteristics. . . . These six [petitions] are found to correspond to the Decalogue and the Two Great Commandments (Mt. 22:40, Mk. 12:31), in that the first half has reference to God, the second half to man. In the first three petitions we seek the glory of our heavenly Father; in the last three the advantage of ourselves and our fellow-men. But these two are closely connected. What is to God's glory benefits His children; and what is to the advantage of men glorifies their heavenly Father. Thus the first half shows the end which man must have in view—the accomplishment of God's glory, kingdom, and will; the second half shows the means—daily provision, forgiveness, and protection. . . .

"And in each of the triplets we can observe progression. The hallowing of God's name leads to the coming of the kingdom; and when the kingdom is come God's will shall be fulfilled on earth as in heaven. In the second half we have first the obtaining of good, and then the removal of evil, past, present, and future. . . . Such exquisite proportion and development . . . are strong evidence that, if this marvellous prayer was constructed out of fragments of other prayers, it was composed in the spirit and power of Him who said, 'Behold, I make all things new' (Rev. 21:5). . . .

"The Lord's Prayer is also a summary of all other prayers. . . . It covers all earthly and spiritual needs and all heavenly aspirations. It is not meant to supersede all other forms of supplication. . . . This one rightly accompanies all other prayers, either following them to sum them up . . . or preceding them as a guide or model."[4]

Well said, Dr. Hastings!

It's been good learning together with you. Through researching and writing this book, and of course praying as I went along, my own knowledge has grown. I hope you will want to go on and apply these truths further, and one way to do this is by using the study material that follows. By now you no doubt have already seen benefits from reflecting on the Lord's Prayer. God is creative, and when you use His prayer as a model for your way of life, you grow in fellowship with Him and the meaning of the prayer deepens and widens. So I encourage you to continue to pray it slowly, listening to God as you go and as you intercede for others. The more involved you get in it, the more results will follow.

Truly the Lord's Prayer is an inner healing prayer. It is a vital starting point and a sustaining support for your wholeness. From here you can pray for further healing, as needed. Jesus taught His disciples to pray, and He is still teaching His disciples, including you and me.

What a different world this would be if everyone used the Lord's Prayer daily! Beginning with you, this is starting to happen. And you can spread the word to others. There are novel ways—how about a bumper sticker on your car asking, "Have you prayed the Lord's Prayer today?" Or teaching a neighborhood or lunchtime-at-the-office Bible study? Or gather a group together to intercede for leaders in government via the Lord's Prayer on the steps of your city hall, state capitol or the nation's Capitol? Best of all, let's also live it so that people will ask, "What's so different about you?" or say, "I feel so peaceful when I'm around you. Take me to your Leader!"

One night while working on this book I went to bed with a particular question on my mind, and I woke up the next morning with this thought, which answered it: *We will reach the world in proportion to the fullness of God we allow in our lives.* I realized again God is calling us to excellence—to making the best use of our time here on earth. The Christian life is not a popularity contest but a life-and-death conflict between heaven and hell. You are needed to help remove the smell of brimstone from this earth, and to bring the fragrance of heaven in its place. Praying the Lord's Prayer and using the other guidelines given here can help you do this. And as you walk in wholeness, more of God can come to you and through you. Put another way, for the Kingdom of God to come through you to the world effectively, you must become whole. God loves you just as you are, but He also wants to help you to be all you can be.

I hope this book has inspired you with new ways to use the Lord's Prayer and brought fresh manna from its Author, Jesus Christ. May these thoughts help you use His prayer, which is also your prayer, just the way He wants and needs you to.

Part 2

15
How to Use This Study Guide

This study is divided into seven sections, each comprising two chapters. Since some chapters are larger than others the teacher should be well-organized in order to do a thorough job on the lessons.

Most groups find it difficult to meet together for more than seven sessions at a time. If preferred, however, a group may take one chapter at a time and do the study in fourteen sessions; the group can then divide the seven sets of questions in half since they were devised with this possibility in mind. For the small prayer and share groups the ten-minute individual exercises are divided into two categories—*a* and *b*—and these also can be divided into fourteen segments.

This Study Guide can be used for a retreat, a seven-week Lenten study or a seminar. It also works well for adult couples or singles groups, teen study groups or home prayer meetings.

*　　*　　*

To get the most out of this Study Guide, I offer the following instructions to the person teaching. (Also, please see Appendices A and B.)

(A) Entire Group Together

Time permitting, begin each meeting with a few songs of praise, 5 to 10 minutes at the most. Study and prayer should have priority.

Before you begin teaching, especially in the first two sessions, give the class a brief overview of activities so they will know what to expect. Using a black or white board, or transparency and overhead projector, can speed this up.

Strive to be well-versed in prayer for inner and outer wholeness. For the first hour, present the lesson that relates to the section being studied, and close with a prayer. You may find it helpful to use the prayer given at the end of the section studied. The teaching and prayer should take not more than 50 or 60 minutes. You may wish to have a leader (facilitator) help you.

If you need assistance in helping others in the small-group sessions, you may find the help you need in my previous books on inner healing and wholeness. (For a book list, see footnote 3 of chapter 2 of the Book Notes, page 209.)

Following the teaching and prayer, *do not break the class.* Each class member should take 5 minutes to read the questions given for that chapter, and *briefly jot down a few thoughts* in their notebooks or on paper you provide.

Then each person should take 10 minutes to do the individual exercise that follows the questions. Make sure the students get a full 10 minutes to do this so they will be ready for the small group work.

(Fifteen minutes is the total individual response time.)

(B) Small Groups of Threes

Divide the group into threes during the first class. If there is good rapport, these same groups should continue to meet together each time. (In working with threes there is no concern about pairing off persons of opposite sex.)

Before gathering in these small groups, you might have a coffee or tea break for 5 or 10 minutes. In the interest of time, class members might bring their refreshments with them to the group.

Meet for 15 minutes to share what's been written or thought about in the individual exercise. Pray for one another when needs surface.

Indicate when the prayer and sharing time is up. It is helpful to use a timer with a bell or a watch with an alarm. Small groups may need more time as they go along, so be observant.

(C) Medium-Sized Discussion Groups of Ten

For 15 or 20 minutes, groups of 10 or fewer will meet with previously selected and knowledgeable group leaders to discuss the questions given. These leaders should be reading ahead in *Inner Wholeness through the Lord's Prayer*. No class member should give input more than once until all have had a chance. Let sharing be spontaneous, not a requirement; remember, the quiet ones may want to share but sometimes need to be encouraged.

(D) Entire Group Together Again

Invite all to come together for the closing. Pray spontaneously, and encourage others to participate also. Try to end on time—taking about two hours in all or, if more time is available, two and a half hours.

16
Study Guide

I. Lord's Prayer "to the Max," Our Father
(*From chapters 1 and 2*)

Take **5** minutes to look over the following questions and then do the **10**-minute individual exercise:

1. Is it hard for you to find time to pray?
   a. Where is the location you have the most success in praying?
   b. Do you feel you need help in knowing how to pray effectively and/or in knowing what to pray about?

2. Do things seem to go better for you when you pray? In what ways?

3. Give a definition of prayer.

4. Approximately how old were you when you learned the Lord's Prayer?
   a. Where did you learn it?
   b. Do you use it only in church or also on your own?

5. Have you ever prayed the Lord's Prayer in a "minimized" way? Describe.

6. Do you feel closer to the Father or to the Son?
   a. Are you comfortable calling God the Father, "Daddy" (Abba)?
   b. Has your relationship with your heavenly Father grown during your life?

7. If you had a negative relationship with your earthly father, can you tell how this may have affected your relationship with God? Reverse this question: If you had a positive relationship with your father. . . ?

8. Did you feel loved by your earthly biological or adoptive father? By a grandfather or brother? If so, how did he show his love?

9. Have you ever had any difficulty praying the Lord's Prayer? Do you understand why?

10. When you don't feel loved by others do you find it helps to think about God's love? Have you tried this?
    a. Jesus said, "As the Father loved Me, I also have loved you; abide in My love" (John 15:9); "I have made you known to them, and will continue to make you known in order that the love you have for me

may be in them and that I myself may be in them"
(John 17:26, NIV).

b. Think about Scriptures such as these especially when
life seems difficult. Another helpful time is when going
to sleep, although any time is good.

10-Minute Individual Exercise:

If you need a review, read and think about the story of the
Prodigal Son in Luke 15:11–32. Reflect especially on the father
speaking kind and affirming words to his son.

Were you ever far away from God? How did you come
back? Hear God the Father speaking these words to you,
His son or His daughter. See Him coming to you with outstretched arms to welcome you home. Write what you see, feel,
hear in your personal meditation time. As God inspires you in
this, the words from Him will be the most loving ones you can
conceive of.

(If you need more help feeling God's love, reread the first
pages of chapter 2, or at another time read *Emotionally Free*, pp.
63–65, 131–138, and *Making Peace with Your Inner Child*, chapters 8 and 9, pages 148–176.)

Meet with your small prayer and share group for 15 minutes,
then the large discussion group for 15 or 20 minutes. You will do
this each time so I won't continue to repeat these instructions.

2. In Heaven, Holy Is Your Name
(*From chapters 3 and 4*)

Take **5** minutes to look over the following questions and then
do the **10**-minute individual exercise:

1. Have you, or has someone you know, died and come back to this life—often called a "near-death experience"? Tell about it.

2. Have you ever been with someone you loved when he or she was dying? Were you able to comfort or pray for or with him/her?

3. Have you ever known near-death experiences to be used to promote the idea that everyone will "make it" to the full Kingdom of heaven regardless of having received Jesus Christ in this life? In what way? Should such wrong usage cause us to discount the real?

4. What Scripture examples do you know that show a decision for Jesus Christ must be made in this life—even if it's in the last seconds of it?

5. Should you judge where a person has gone after death, or leave the judgment up to God?

6. In the past have you been offended at profanity in a movie, a play or while reading a book? (*Profanity* means any use of God's name—Father, Son or Holy Spirit—in a degrading way.) What did you do? Would you do anything differently today?

7. What is the best way to handle exposure to heavy profanity? On the job? In the home? At school? Elsewhere?

8. Did a parent, sibling or mate ever abuse you with profane or obscene words? If so, at your earliest convenience, ask

God to cleanse and heal the effect of verbal abuse on your memories, conscious and subconscious. (Have some people join you in prayer if you need help doing this. Wait in His presence for Him to replace evil names you were called with loving words or names.)

9. Do you have, or have you had, a habit of using profanity? Obscenity? (*Obscenity* here means vulgar words used without God's name.) How can you, or how did you, help yourself overcome this habit?

10. Which of the ten descriptive attributes of God is most meaningful to you?

   During your times of quiet reflection, or when you awaken in the night, do you ever meditate on God's omnipresence above you, beside you, around you, within you, and His unconditional love for you?

10-Minute Individual Exercise:

Write God a letter about any needs these questions have brought to mind. Be honest about your feelings.

Or write a letter of thanks to someone who did something kind for you. You may want to mail it later.

When you meet together with your small prayer and share group, and just before you begin discussing what you've written, join hands and pray spontaneously a personalized Lord's Prayer inserting one of your partners' names. Be sensitive as you pray, and don't rush.

Reverse and let the other person pray it for you. Go around the triad until each has experienced praying and being prayed for

Don't worry about following the suggested prayer perfectly. Trust your memory and the Holy Spirit. If you need help preparing for this, turn to the section "Praying the Lord's Prayer for Someone Else" in chapter 14.

3. Your Kingdom Come, Your Will Be Done
(From chapters 5 and 6)

Take **5** minutes to look over the following questions and then do the **10**-minute individual exercise:

1. How does God go about setting up His Kingdom on earth?
   a. Do you believe you have His Kingdom within you?
   b. When did you first know this was so?

2. What are some of the ways you can recognize God's Kingdom? What are some ways you can promote it?

3. What are you doing, or have you done, to help change your world for the better?

4. What are some of the kind actions you've experienced from others that show the Kingdom kind of living?

5. Should we continue to pray for God's Kingdom to come to earth? Give two reasons. Why is it important to view God's Kingdom in three dimensions?

6. Have you ever felt your will was smashed by an authority figure? Explain, if you feel comfortable. Did someone tell you no excessively when you were a child of two or three?

7. Are you afraid that if you were to say to God, "Your will be done," He would surely ask you to do something you don't want to do, or send you to a place where you don't want to live?

8. Are you sure God wants good things for you? Since His will is that earth be the same as heaven, do you think that includes your entering into these benefits?

9. Have you ever tried saying out loud what you know the will of God is for you? How does this make you feel? (Meditate on Mark 11:23–24.) Would you rather be around a negative person or a positive person?

10. On a scale from 1 to 10, where would you see your will in relation to being passive/aggressive? Do you feel you are balanced? Is there a need for prayer?

10-Minute Individual Exercise:

Write a letter to God about where you are in yielding your will to Him. If you have a high level of trust, tell Him about it. Share why you may be gifted in this way (for example, a happy childhood or consistent parental love, especially in your infancy).

Or, if you're afraid or hesitant at all about praying that "God's will be done" in your life, share that and give any reasons why you may feel this way. (If you need prayer, ask for it during your small group sharing.)

4. On Earth As It Is in Heaven, Give Us This Day Our Daily Bread
(*From chapters 7 and 8*)

Take **5** minutes to look over the following questions and then do the **10**-minute individual exercise:

1. Can you see the value in working persistently in the direction of health both supernaturally through prayer and in natural ways? Can you think of scriptural or personal examples of persistence?

2. Have you ever been to a medical doctor who witnessed to you about Jesus or his faith in God, or who prayed with you for healing?

3. What three things should you do when you're healed through prayer?

4. Have you ever prayed for a sick person or an animal and seen an immediate healing, or a faster recovery than was expected?

5. Have you ever been healed through prayer? Describe it.

6. God sent food to the children of Israel for forty years. He provided food three times for the prophet Elijah: when God commanded the ravens to feed him meat and bread, when angels gave him water and baked him two cakes that nourished him forty days, and when the widow's last oil and meal were fed him and then God multiplied it to her, her son and Elijah (her houseguest), throughout a three-year famine (1 Kings 17–19).

We always need to remember that God can do the impossible, yet He normally works through human beings to help human beings. Have you ever taken a basket of food to a needy family at Christmas, Easter, Thanksgiving or at other times?

a. What was their response? How did you feel?

b. Have you fed a needy person in your home or given money to others to feed the hungry?

7. Have you ever been in a situation in which you had to be concerned where your next meal was coming from? Were you a committed Christian at the time? What did you do? What did God do?

8. Are you taking as good care of your body as you are of your home or car?

a. Have you read a book on nutrition during the past five years?

b. Do you have a regular pattern of exercise?

9. After you have done what you can to make plans for the future, does it help you to remember to put your plans at Jesus' feet, take a deep breath and rest in His presence?

a. What are some of the wrong ways you have dealt with stress in the past?

b. What are some of the positive things you can do to cope with stress?

c. Do you feed on His Word daily, either by reading or by memory?

d. Do you get good spiritual fellowship?

10. What kinds of things make you anxious—being late to meetings, deadlines on office or schoolwork, paying your

bills on time, children (parents) out late, etc.? Do you take time to get away from your routine to receive concentrated spiritual nurture at least once a year? If not, why not?

10-Minute Individual Exercise:

If you are anxious and don't know why, ask God to give you wisdom to know where to look for the root cause. Make a circle and write *anxious* (or *stressed*) in it, then make spokes around it and write on them the things you are anxious about. Realize Jesus is with you to help you. Now say to yourself, "I've done the best I know, so with God's help I choose not to be anxious. I will live one day at a time." Say to yourself several times, "Be anxious for nothing, but in everything by prayer and supplication, with thanksgiving, let your requests be made known to God" (Philippians 4:6). As you quote this take a deep breath; if your hands are closed, open them; let the tension go. Give each anxiety to Him. (See 1 Peter 5:7.)

If the preceding doesn't apply to you at this time because you are free from anxiety or worry, do the following exercise instead. Picture yourself jogging, walking, running, skiing on snow or water, camping, gazing at the stars at night; and then write a reflected Lord's Prayer in this setting. For an example, recall my snorkeling experience from chapter 10.

5. Forgive Us Our Sins As We Forgive Those Who Sin Against Us
(*From chapters 9 and 10*)

Take 5 minutes to look over the following questions and then do the 10-minute individual exercise:

1. Why is it important to know the difference between "original sin," which is the spirit being out of action or "dead to God" due to separation from Him, and "daily sins" which are sins of the soul resulting from that separation?

   What could be the result if a person knew he couldn't forgive someone from his soul's emotions and he believed the Father would totally reject him on account of it?

2. Can you think of a time when you repented from the "little deaths" of sins, asking God to forgive you, and then felt "resurrection life" well up inside you? If you feel free to share, do so.

3. Do you make it a practice to confess all known sins to God before going to sleep at night? If married, do you try to reconcile everything with your mate before going to sleep? With your children?

4. Have you ever asked a person to forgive you? Was it hard to do? Were you glad you did?

5. Describe how you can tell when you've really forgiven another.
   a. If a person continues year after year to tell people about another's sins against him or her, do you think he or she has forgiven that person?
   b. Have you ever said, "I will never forgive _____"? Have you prayed about this?

6. Describe a situation where it was hard to forgive but you were finally able to do so. (Be careful when sharing not to reveal the identity of the one you forgave, unless the story

has been publicly shared by that person, or you are *positive* he/she wouldn't mind.)

7. Have you ever been hit by "soft rocks" as Pat (young Patty) was?
   a. How did you finally discover them and their identity? How many years did it take?
   b. Have you been able to forgive the thrower(s) of the "rocks"?

8. Have you been able to forgive with your will even when you could only say, "I want to want to forgive, dear Lord"? (In the light of Jesus' prayer, be sure your forgiveness account is cleared daily.)

9. Have you ever prayed by yourself, or had others pray with you, to enable you to forgive someone else from the level of your emotions?
   a. What was most helpful to you?
   b. Were the effects of this way to forgive long-lasting?
   c. Did it take a few days or months to work through your feelings before being able to do this?

10. Have you been unable to forgive yourself for sins of the past that you know God promised to forgive when you asked Him, but you still hold against yourself?

10-Minute Individual Exercise:

Royal Forgiveness:
Remember Dawn's and Lou's stories. God is reigning in you also; you are a redeemed child of God. Through Jesus Christ you

have been made a king or a queen, a prince or a princess. Picture yourself as royalty and then think of someone you need to forgive. See him come into the throne room. Note the generous way you greet him. What does he say? How does he stand and how does he look at you? How do you respond? Write down your experience.

Now see yourself as a penniless beggar. See the person you need to forgive. What does he say? How does he act? How do you respond? Is it harder to forgive in this role? Note how this feels.

Go back to the regal scene, and with Jesus, the King of kings, there to support you, forgive the person more completely. Write your experiences.

Share what you wrote with your small prayer group. If you need help with something that surfaced, do so. If your need is too personal, ask the teacher to recommend a team to pray for you later.

6. Lead Us Not into Temptation, But Deliver Us from Evil
(*From chapters 11 and 12*)

Take **5** minutes to look over the following questions and then do the **10**-minute individual exercise:

1. Does Jesus tell you not to sin, and then try to lead you into temptation to sin? Would you ever lead your children or brothers or sisters into temptation?

2. Do you remember a time when you were tempted but found a way of escape? (My New York experience is an example. First Corinthians 10:13 tells about a way of escape.)
   a. Did you take the way of escape? Or were you not willing or able to act soon enough?

b. What helps you most in resisting temptation?

3. Does temptation come only to the young or do you think it comes appropriately camouflaged for each decade of life? Do you think youths usually have fewer tools with which to handle temptations than do adults?

4. Recognizing the differences between temptation, tribulation and testing, and using the checklist given, can you think of a time when God acted as a good and helpful Teacher by giving you a test of your Christian skills? (See examples: Matthew 15:21–28 and John 6:5–6.)

5. When and how do temptations become sins?

6. From what three directions do temptations come?

7. Describe a time when you discerned evil in a person(s) or in a location, although others around you were not aware of it.

8. Have you, or has anyone you know, ever received deliverance prayer?
   a. Have you ever helped set a person free who was in spiritual captivity?
   b. What did you do?

9. God's Word gives us pictures of pieces of armor to describe our protection. Why do you think He did it this way rather than simply explaining it to us in concepts? In what way(s) have you found this teaching helpful?

10. Do you find it helpful to visualize putting on the whole armor of God daily as Paul said to do? Have you tried doing this in conjunction with praying the reflected Lord's Prayer?

   a. Do you claim the protection of Jesus' blood over your life and your household, including your transportation, on a daily basis?

   b. Though you can't possibly know all God has done to protect you, do you find that things are going better for you and your household since praying this way? Describe.

10-Minute Individual Exercise:

Write a prayer to assist you in putting on the whole armor of God, based on the verses of Ephesians 6:10–18. Take time to thank God in writing or in silent prayer for His protection in your life in a specific manner and for His angels who have kept charge over you.

Or, if there are some situations in which you did not seem to be protected in your past, write a letter to God about it. Ask Him to show you how aid was hindered from getting to you. Were unforgiveness or other sins making you vulnerable to the enemy's "fiery darts"? If you have blamed God and been angry with Him, tell Him about it. When through, receive His love and forgiveness.

7. The Doxology of the Lord's Prayer and Intercessory Prayer
(*From chapters 13 and 14*)

Take **5** minutes to look over the following questions and then do the **10**-minute individual exercise:

1. Have you ever been hurt by people who were building their own kingdoms?
   a. What did you do? Withdraw quietly? Confront? Pray about it? Ask counsel? (Share, keeping names confidential.)
   b. Have you hurt people with your own kingdom-building? Have you asked them to forgive you? Have you prayed about it?

2. Can you think of a time when Jesus' *exousia* authority was expressed through you? His *dunamis* power? When you're not feeling confident, do you find it harder to speak in God's loving but definite authority?

3. Have you ever seen a person's face shining with God's glow and glory as they were talking about God or praising God? Describe.

4. Do you try each day to praise God "in the Spirit" and "with the understanding" as you drive, wash dishes, jog, shower? If spontaneous praise is not easy for you, memorize phrases from the Psalms or quote hymns that are full of praise.

5. Where have you found it easiest to pray the Lord's Prayer reflectively?
   a. Have you found it best for you to do it in shifts?
   b. Has it been difficult for you to find time to pray this way?

6. Have you been able to add intercessions to the Lord's Prayer? Are you finding this easier to do—say, on the

weekend—when you have more time, or are you able to do it daily?

7. Have you been able to add a quiet time of listening and receiving at the end of your intercessions?
   a. Have you tried to keep a journal of what you feel the Lord has said to you?
   b. During this time have you also received Scriptures or *rhema* words from Scripture? Share some.

8. What are some of the results you have been experiencing since praying the Lord's Prayer reflectively? "To the max"?

9. Is it becoming easier for you to reach the goal of being a one-hundred-percent forgiver?

10. Is there anyone you consciously have not forgiven?
    Would you like individual prayer for this? Ask your small prayer and share group to help you, or request that a prayer team meet with you.

10-Minute Individual Exercise:

For review, write down how this class has helped you with your prayer life. Write what activity you have enjoyed the most. You might want also to mail this to the teacher to encourage him or her.

Or, express on paper some words of praise and thanksgiving to God for how He has helped you now and in the past.

As time permits, say the Lord's Prayer slowly, reflecting on what you have learned during these studies.

To the Teacher:

After the small prayer and sharing group, and the larger discussion group, meet back together with the entire large group—as you have done each session.

This time conclude the class by building a reflective, personalized Lord's Prayer together. Repeat the individual Scripture phrases and let the class members, as so inspired, pray along those topics until the prayer is completed. Time permitting, have intercessory prayers for those the group is concerned about.

If your group enjoys singing, then join hands in a circle, or while hands are joined, lift them and sing the Lord's Prayer. Hug your brothers and sisters in Christ and know that you will never be the same after experiencing this little bit of heaven on earth!

Appendix A: Questions Concerning Use of the Lord's Prayer

Who would ever dream there could be objections to using the Lord's Prayer? Yet I know of several that have been shared widely.

First, some believe it is an Old Covenant, Old Testament prayer, no longer applicable today. They say that since God's Kingdom has already come through Jesus Christ and in His people, it is no longer necessary to pray, "Thy Kingdom come." They also say that since Jesus told us to make our requests to the Father in His (Jesus') name, this confirms that it is an Old Testament, pre-Christian prayer. I have already answered these objections thoroughly in this book, so I won't repeat those answers here.

I realize teachers like to shock students to make them think, and I believe that's what some of these fine people are doing by challenging us on the use of the Lord's Prayer. I am sure they themselves try to live by the teachings of the prayer, whether they use it personally or not.

I most sincerely believe Jesus' prayer is of great value today; yet I know, too, that God truly loves all His children regardless of our varying opinions. Your entrance into heaven certainly won't be based on whether you pray the Lord's Prayer or not. There's no need to spoil it, however, for those who find strength and blessing in it. As for me, I find great inspiration and illumination in using His prayer as a guide to my own prayer life. When I see Jesus and if He asks, "What did you think of the prayer I left you?" I'm going to hug His neck and say, "It was fantastic, Lord!"

Another Concern

Some people suggest we change the language of the Lord's Prayer to be "inclusive," which means that, when speaking of God, we should use words that can apply to both male and female, not excluding one or the other. It is proposed, for example, that instead of *Father* we could call God *Creator, Comforter, Father/Mother God* or sometimes even *Mother.*

Inclusivists reason that since women are not inferior to men, and since God is neither male nor female, and since many people have a negative picture of *father,* it's kinder to make God a more in-between sort of Being. I acknowledged and addressed "father problems" in the second chapter of this book. It seems to me the question is, Are we going to let our picture of God be in agreement with the Scriptures, or are we going to adjust the Scriptures to ease our damaged emotions? Surely a better way to handle the situation would be to get healed from our soul hurts, so we can love God for who He is, the truly wonderful father (as well as a symbol of a nurturing mother), rather than try to emasculate Him.

Appendix A

Disciples' Prayer or Lord's Prayer?

Another fairly well-known problem is not one of usage, but of proper entitling. Some say the Lord's Prayer should be called the Disciples' Prayer instead, since Jesus Christ gave it to His disciples to use. "Why should we call it the *Lord's* Prayer unless He used this prayer Himself?" they ask.

I understand their concern, but to call it the Disciples' Prayer is confusing since it seems to indicate the disciples composed it.

Did Jesus use His own prayer? He could have, except for one part—that is, "Forgive us our sins, as we forgive those who sin against us," for He "was in all points tempted like as we are, yet without sin" (Hebrews 4:15, KJV). But whether He prayed it or not doesn't affect its importance to us, for all the truths in it were taught by Him. So I think this great prayer should bear the Author's name in its title, rather than the name of those for whom it was given.

For those who have been concerned about some or all of these issues, I hope my comments will bring clarification and understanding.

Appendix B: Creative Imagination and Prayer

During this class the question of visualizing may come up because of the New Age and cultish misuse of God's gifts.

It is always good to define terms. New Age visualizing is attempting to use the mind to manipulate circumstances and the world for self-centered purposes. This is clearly outside the work of the Holy Spirit. Christian visualizing in prayer is allowing God to use your creative imagination to illumine you with the truth of His Word, and as a result draw you closer to Him—Father, Son and Holy Spirit.

For more information and clarification on this, write to Christian Renewal Association, P.O. Box 576, Edmonds, WA 98020, and ask for the booklet *Seeing by Faith* by Dennis and Rita Bennett.

Book Notes

Chapter 1

[1]Fr. Alphonsus Liguori, 1696–1787.

[2]Scriptures showing Jesus Christ as the Creator-God: John 1:3; 1 Corinthians 8:6; Ephesians 3:9; Colossians 1:16; Hebrews 1:2.

[3]For a detailed and scholarly explanation about dating Matthew's account see:

James Hastings, M.A., D.D., editor, *A Dictionary of the Bible* (New York: Charles Scribner's Sons, 1900), p. 141.

[4]Massey Hamilton Shepherd, Jr., *The Oxford American Prayer Book Commentary* (New York: Oxford University Press, Inc., 1950), pp. 81–82.

Dr. Shepherd also says about the Lord's Prayer: "It sums up the intention of the whole liturgy, with respect to both the larger purpose of God for the consummation of His Kingdom and to the immediate strengthening of His people in fulfilling His will day by day. Its use in the Eucharistic liturgy can be traced back to the fourth century" (p. 81–82).

[5]Hastings, *A Dictionary of the Bible,* Vol. III, p. 143.

[6]*The Book of Common Prayer* (New York: The Church Hymnal Corporation, 1979), p. 364.

[7]The historic liturgical churches honor the Lord's Prayer with consistent use and give it precedence at special points in the service. *Liturgy* means any agreed pattern of worship in which each person has an understood part to play. Every church group that has a consistent way of doing things, and in which the leaders and people participate in an agreed manner, is using a liturgy. Some parts of Christian liturgies have been in use for thousands of years, as they came from the worship of ancient Israel.

Chapter 2

[1]This illustration came from the Rev. George Baybrook, many years pastor of the Wailuku Union Church in Wailuku, Maui. While in seminary in 1962, he participated in a supervised clinical training program at Danvers State Mental Hospital outside Boston. He was impressed by this statement made by the chaplain.

[2]Most translations of Proverbs 17:6 say in various ways that the father is the glory of the children:

"The glory of children are their fathers" (KJV); "And the glory of children is their father" (NKJV); "The children's glory is their father" (JERUSALEM BIBLE); "A child's glory is his father" (LB); "The glory of children is their fathers" (AMERICAN BIBLE).

The American Standard Bible says, "And the glory of sons is their fathers."

The New International Version includes both parents: "Parents are the pride of their children."

[3]Here is a list of my own books on inner healing (there are, of course, other authors whose books can assist you, too): *You Can Be Emotionally Free; Making Peace with Your Inner Child; How to Pray for Inner Healing for Yourself and Others* by Rita Bennett, published by Fleming H. Revell Co., Old Tappan, New Jersey 07675. Also *Trinity of Man* by Dennis and Rita Bennett, published by New Leaf Press, Green Forest, AR 72638.

[4]Aramaic, although not a derivative or dialect of Hebrew, is a member of the same family of languages. Jesus was undoubtedly familiar with both Hebrew and Aramaic, and *Abba,* the word for "Daddy," was the same in both.

"If Greek was the language of the court and camp, and indeed must have been understood and spoken by most in the land, the language of the people, spoken also by Christ and His Apostles, was . . . Aramaic."

Alfred Edersheim, *The Life and Times of Jesus the Messiah* (Wm. B. Eerdmans Publishing Co., Grand Rapids, Mich.), one-volume edition, Nov. 1971, Part One, p. 129.

"That He [Jesus] spoke Hebrew, and used and quoted the Scriptures in the original, has already been shown, although, no doubt, He understood Greek, possibly also Latin."

The Life and Times of Jesus the Messiah, Part One, pp. 252–253.

[5]Dake in his *Annotated Bible* says, "Each angel could slay 185,000 in a night, as one did in Isaiah 37:36. On this basis, 13,320,000,000 or 11 billion more men than there are now on earth could easily have been killed."

Finis Jennings Dake, *Dake's Annotated Reference Bible* (Atlanta: Dake Bible Publishers), 1963, p. 31.

[6]Our current population and therefore calculations are a little different from Mr. Dake's made in 1963. An update on the earth's population in 1989 was 5 billion 192 thousand (5,000,192,000). Figures are from the Seattle Public Library, quick information department.

[7]Charles M. Laymon, editor, *The Interpreter's One-Volume Commentary on the Bible* (Nashville and New York: Abingdon Press, 1971) p. 783.

Chapter 3

[1]J. D. Douglas, organizing editor, *The New Bible Dictionary* (Grand Rapids, Mich.: Wm. B. Eerdmans Publishing Co., 1962), p. 510.

See a few helpful references defining heaven: "The abode of God (Gen. 28:17; Ps. 80:14; Is. 66:1; Matt. 5:12) and of the good angels (Matt. 24:36); where the redeemed shall someday be (Matt. 5:12; 6:20; Eph. 3:15); where the Redeemer has gone and intercedes for the saints, and from which He will someday come for His own (I Thess. 4:16)." Merrill C. Tenney, gen. ed., *The Zondervan Pictorial Bible Dictionary* (Grand Rapids, Mich.: Zondervan Publishing House, 1963), p. 340.

[2]The word here translated "nations" usually means "foreigners," "heathen" or Gentiles. Perhaps this means that as people arrive they will be healed, or perhaps it speaks of the healing power of heaven going out into the earth through the Holy Spirit. It may indicate both.

[3]C. S. Lewis, *The Voyage of the Dawn Treader* (Harmondsworth, Middlesex, England: Penguin Books Ltd., 1952), pp. 193–195.

C. S. Lewis, *The Last Battle* (New York: Macmillan Publishing Co., Inc., 1956), p. 137.

Born in Northern Ireland, the late Professor Clive Staples Lewis taught at Oxford and later at Cambridge University. He has probably done more than any other modern author to provide both adults and children with an easy-to-understand presentation of the Christian faith. His children's masterpiece is undoubtedly this seven-book series, *The Chronicles of Narnia*. In the Narnia series, along with the three books of his "Space Trilogy," he stretches our imaginations in picturing God and His Kingdom.

[4]This idea is drawn from C. S. Lewis, *The Silver Chair* (New York. Macmillan Publishing Co., Inc., 1953), p. 213.

[5] "A True Adventure," by Phil (Filipe) Saint, *Christian Life* magazine, July 1983, p. 55.

[6] "Death Trip," by Marvin Barrett, *Lear's* magazine, November 1989.

[7] This thought was adapted from C. S. Lewis, *The Last Battle* (New York: Macmillan Publishing Co., Inc., 1956), p. 148.

[8] C. S. Lewis, *The Great Divorce* (New York: Macmillan Publishing Co., Inc., 1946).

[9] The Bible is nearly silent in telling us where heaven is located. Some people feel it is totally silent. Others say that Isaiah 14:12–14 can be taken to be a reference, since Lucifer, the fallen archangel who wanted to take the throne away from God, said, "I will sit also upon the mount of the congregation, in the sides of the north." In other words, "I will be as God, or will be God, and rule the universe!" Another is Psalm 75:6, which says, "For promotion cometh neither from the east, nor from the west, nor from the south. But God is the judge: he putteth down one, and setteth up another"(both references from kjv). It is inferred that since promotion from God comes from the north, that must therefore be where heaven is. But what way is north when you get away from this little planet earth? *North* has meaning only in terms of this world.

Heaven is a real place; Jesus speaks of it as so. But for finite human beings to try to locate and limit it in terms of space and time is probably a fruitless task. For now, all we need to know is that heaven is wherever God is known, loved and obeyed.

Chapter 4

[1] Henry Bosley Woolf, ed. in chief, *Webster's New Collegiate Dictionary* (Springfield, Mass.: G. & C. Merriam Co., 1979), pp. 523, 542, 1328.

In French, *sain* means "whole or healthy, sane, wholesome, safe."

Book Notes

In German, *heil* means "safe, cured, healed." *Heilig* means "holy." To be holy is to be whole.

²Woolf, pp. 542, 1328, 523.

³Merrill C. Tenney, gen. ed., *The Zondervan Pictorial Bible Dictionary* (Grand Rapids, Mich.: Zondervan Publishing House, 1963), p. 357:

"Holiness, Holy, usually translate words derived from a Heb. root *qadash* and Greek *hag-*. The basic meaning of *qadash* is separateness, withdrawal. It is first applied to God, and is early associated with ideas of purity and righteousness. . . . Greek *hag-* is an equivalent of *qadash* and its history is similar. Beginning as an attribute of deity the *hag-* family of words developed two stems, one meaning 'holy,' the other 'pure.' The use of words of this family in the LXX to translate the *qadash* family resulted in a great development of their ethical sense, which was never clear in classical Greek. What became increasingly evident in the OT is overwhelmingly explicit in the NT: that holiness means the pure, loving nature of God, separate from evil, aggressively seeking to universalize itself; that this character inheres in places, times and institutions intimately associated with worship; and that it is to characterize human beings who have entered into personal relations with God."

⁴"Summary: the idea of holiness originates in the revealed character of God, and is communicated to things, places, times and persons engaged in His service. . . . Holiness is interwoven with righteousness and purity. To seek holiness apart from the other qualities of a Christlike life is to wander from the way of holiness itself." *The Zondervan Pictorial Bible Dictionary*, p. 358.

⁵*The Zondervan Pictorial Bible Dictionary*, p. 408.

⁶Here I'm using the rendering of the King James Version of the Bible. Other Bible translations write these four Hebrew consonants a little differently. For example, *Strong's Exhaustive Concordance of the*

214

Bible in its dictionary uses: Yôwd, Hê´, Vâv, Hê´.

James Strong, S.T.D., LL. D., *Strong's Exhaustive Concordance of the Bible, A Concise Dictionary of the Words in the Hebrew Bible* (Nashville and New York: Abingdon-Cokesbury Press, 1890), p. 5.

It may also be interesting to note that there are 22 letters regarded as consonants in the Hebrew alphabet. There were originally no vowels as such, although much later in history, vowel points were provided. Translators took the vowels of *Adhonai* and inserted them into the word *JHVH,* and came up with *Jehovah.* Later scholars theorized that the word should be *Jahweh* or *Yahweh.*

[7]Tetragrammaton: "The four Hebrew letters usually transliterated YHWH or JHVH form a biblical proper name of God." *Webster's New Collegiate Dictionary,* p. 1197.

[8]*The Zondervan Pictorial Bible Dictionary,* p. 408.

[9]This is a transposition of the quote from Søren Kierkegaard. John Bartlett, *Bartlett's Familiar Quotations*, 14th Edition (Boston and Toronto: Little, Brown and Co., 1882), p. 552.

[10]*The Zondervan Pictorial Bible Dictionary,* p. 751.

[11]The article referred to is available in a pamphlet called "Soul Restoration via Psalm 23." This pamphlet and *The Morning Watch* newsletter are both available from Christian Renewal Association, Inc., P.O. Box 576, Edmonds, WA 98020.

[12]Rita Bennett, *Emotionally Free* (Old Tappan, N.J.: Fleming H. Revell Co., 1982), p. 52–53.

[13]"In Is. xi. 12 the Messiah is said to raise up such a standard, while in verse 10 He is Himself said to be one. Perhaps this latter reference is intended to be a link with Jehovah-nissi ('The Lord is my Banner') in Ex. xvii. 15."

J. D. Douglas, *The New Bible Dictionary* (Grand Rapids, Mich., Wm. B. Eerdmans Publishing Co., 1962), p. 130.

[14]Finis Jennings Dake, *Dake's Annotated Reference Bible* (Atlanta: Dake Bible Publishers), 1963, p. 12.

[15]Other verses you may want to refer to are Genesis 14:18; Daniel 4:17; Psalm 7:17, 47:2; Acts 17:26.

There are actually sixteen or seventeen Hebrew titles for God, but I have listed ten because the others overlap the attributes already given. The form *El Shaddai* is popular with some today; it is usually translated "God Almighty." It comes from a Hebrew root meaning "powerful." It may be related to the Hebrew word *shadu* or mountain, and therefore connected with heights, storms and thunder.

[16]*The Zondervan Pictorial Bible Dictionary*, p. 609.

Chapter 5

[1]"While Matthew, who addresses himself to the Jews, speaks for the most part of the 'kingdom of heaven', Mark and Luke speak of the 'kingdom of God', which has the same meaning as the 'kingdom of heaven', but was more intelligible to non-Jews. The use of 'kingdom of heaven' in Matthew is certainly due to the tendency in Judaism to avoid the direct use of the name of God. In any case no distinction in sense is to be assumed between the two expressions (*cf.*, *e.g.*, Mt. v. 3 with Lk. vi. 20)." J. D. Douglas, *The New Bible Dictionary* (Grand Rapids, Mich.: Wm. B. Eerdmans Publishing Co., 1962), p. 693.

[2]*The New Bible Dictionary*, p. 693.

[3]*The New Bible Dictionary*, pp. 694, 695.

[4]*The New Bible Dictionary*, p. 694.

[5]*The New Bible Dictionary*, p. 694.

[6]George Arthur Buttrick, commentary editor, *The Interpreter's Bible* (Nashville: Abingdon Publishing Co., 1951), p. 312.

[7]*The Interpreter's Bible*, p. 86.

Chapter 6

[1]C. S. Lewis, *The Great Divorce* (New York: Macmillan Publishing Co., Inc., 1946) p. 69.

[2]Adam Clarke (circa 1830), *Clarke's Commentary*, Vol. I (Nashville: Abingdon), p. 86.

[3]Rita Bennett, *How to Pray for Inner Healing for Yourself and Others* (Old Tappan, N.J.: Fleming H. Revell Co., 1984), pp. 67–68.

[4]*Clarke's Commentary*, Vol. I, p. 86.

[5]Saint Augustine of Hippo, *Nicene and Post-Nicene Fathers,* edited by Philip Schaff, D.D. LL.D., Vol. I (Grand Rapids, Mich.: Wm. B. Eerdmans Publishing Co., 1956), p. 45.

[6]Dennis and Rita Bennett, *Trinity of Man* (Green Forest, Ark.: New Leaf Press, 1987), p. 120. See entire chapter for further study on the human will. (This book was first published in 1979 by Logos.)

Chapter 7

[1]Christian Medical Foundation International, founded by Dr. W. S. Reed in 1961, has annual meetings with members of the medical profession to share information on healing through prayer and through medicine. The address is 7522 N. Himes Ave., Tampa, FL 33614.

Chapter 8

[1]William F. Arndt and F. Wilbur Gingrich, *A Greek-English Lexicon of the New Testament and Other Early Christian Literature* (Chicago: The University of Chicago Press, 1957), p. 297.

[2]George Arthur Buttrick, *The Interpreter's Bible*, Vol. VII (Nashville: Abingdon Publishing Co., 1951), p. 312.

[3]*The Interpreter's Bible*, p. 313.

[4]*The Interpreter's Bible*, p. 313.

Chapter 9

[1]Dr. Philip Schaff, editor, *A Select Library of the Nicene and Post-Nicene Fathers*, First Series Vol. III (Grand Rapids, Mich.: Wm. B. Eerdmans Publishing Co., 1956), p. 274.

[2]The Rev. Everett L. Fullam in his book *Living the Lord's Prayer* (Chosen Books, Old Tappan, N.J.) shows that in the New Testament there are five Greek words used to speak of sin with slightly different meanings.

[3]William F. Arndt and F. Wilbur Gingrich, *A Greek-English Lexicon of the New Testament and Other Early Christian Literature* (Chicago: The University of Chicago Press, 1957), pp. 42–43.

Chapter 10

[1]George Arthur Buttrick, *The Interpreter's Bible*, Vol. VII (Nashville: Abingdon Publishing Co., 1951), p. 314.

[2]*Analytical Greek Lexicon* (New York: Harper & Brothers, n.d.), p. 52.

[3]Merrill C. Tenney, gen. ed., *The Zondervan Pictorial Bible Dictionary* (Grand Rapids, Mich.: Zondervan Publishing House, 1963), p. 609.

[4]*Webster's New Collegiate Dictionary*, p. 447.

[5]Rita Bennett, *Making Peace with Your Inner Child* (Old Tappan, N.J.: Fleming H. Revell Co., 1988), pp. 159–160.

[6]Actual hell is final and total separation from God, for those who will not love Him.

Chapter 11

[1]Gerhard Kittel and Gerhard Friedrich, editors, and Geoffrey W. Bromiley, D. Litt., D.D., translator, *Theological Dictionary of the New*

Testament, Vol. VI (Grand Rapids, Mich.: Wm. B. Eerdmans Publishing Co., 1968), p. 31.

[2]George Arthur Buttrick, *The Interpreter's Bible* (Nashville: Abingdon Publishing Co., 1951), p. 314.

[3]Kittel and Friedrich, *Theological Dictionary*, loc. cit.

[4]William F. Arndt and F. Wilbur Gingrich, *A Greek-English Lexicon* (Chicago: The University of Chicago Press, 1957), p. 751.

[5]Charles Capps, *How You Can Avoid Tragedy and Live a Better Life* (Tulsa, Ok.: Harrison House, Inc., 1980), p. 95.

[6]Capps, p. 88.

[7]Adam Clark, *Clarke's Commentary*, Vol. I (Nashville: Abingdon Publishing Co., 1830), pp. 87–88.

[8]For help in praying for deliverance, see *The Holy Spirit and You* by Dennis and Rita Bennett (S. Plainfield, N.J.: Bridge Publishing Co., Inc., 1971).

Chapter 12

[1]Rita Bennett, *How to Put On the Whole Armor of God* (Edmonds, Wash.: Christian Renewal Association, Inc., 1984), Renewal Pamphlet #2, 18 pages. I have excerpted parts of this pamphlet in these opening paragraphs, later in the listing of the armor, and the armor summed up in Jesus; you may obtain the entire teaching by writing us at P. O. Box 576, Edmonds, WA 98020.

[2]Clarke, *Commentary*, Vol. I, p. 436.

[3]The New International Version, New Jerusalem, New King James, Living Bible, Amplified and New English Bible translate this, "Deliver [or save] us from the evil one." The Living Bible capitalizes evil one.

[4]Clarke, *Commentary*, Vol. I, p. 88.

[5]Gerhard Kittel and Gerhard Friedrich, *Theological Dictionary of the New Testament,* Vol. V (Grand Rapids, Mich.: Wm. B. Eerdmans Publishing Co., 1968), pp. 308–309.

See also Dake, *Annotated Reference Bible,* New Testament section, p. 212.

[6]During my research I found the June/July 1981 issue of the magazine *Israel, My Glory* most helpful for an overview of the six pieces of the armor of God. (Published by The Friends of Israel, P. O. Box 123, W. Collingswood, NJ 08107.)

[7]To help you better distinguish between soul and spirit, I suggest you read Dennis and Rita Bennett, *Trinity of Man* (Green Forest, Ark.: New Leaf Press, 1987).

[8]For more help on this read Dennis and Rita Bennett, *The Holy Spirit and You.*

[9]H. B. Garlock, *Before We Kill and Eat You* (Dallas, Texas: Christ for the Nations, 1974), p. 100.

[10]George Arthur Buttrick, *The Interpreter's Bible,* Vol. VII (Nashville: Abingdon Publishing Co., 1951), p. 315.

Chapter 13

[1]The New King James, The Amplified, The New American Standard Bible and perhaps others, put the doxology at the end of the Lord's Prayer in the text; some do so with footnotes about its being added later. Other modern translations do not list it at all.

[2]George Arthur Buttrick, *The Interpreter's Bible,* Vol. VII (Nashville: Abingdon Publishing Co., 1951), p. 315.

[3]Conrad Bennett is a banker and songwriter. His music ministry is "Ministry in Song," 4102 185th St. S. W., Lynnwood, WA 98037.

[4]*The Interpreter's Bible,* Vol. VII, p. 316.

[5]Many of the older versions of the Bible did not make a differentiation between the Greek words for "power" and "authority." I'm glad to see the New International Version, the New King James, and most other new versions do.

[6]*The Interpreter's Bible*, p. 316.

Chapter 14

[1]The Rev. Canon Clifton A. Best, D.D., *The Technique of Prayer or Eight Steps into the Consciousness of God's Presence* (Bellefonte, Pa.: The Chi Rho Center, n.d.). This eight-page pamphlet has been helpful to me over the past several years. I received permission from Mrs. Ruth Best to share some of her husband's inspirational thoughts with you

[2]Best, pp. 5–6.

[3]I learned this concept, which I have adapted, from a woman who shared with me during one of our seminars; I'm sorry that I can't remember her name to give her credit.

[4]James Hastings, editor, *A Dictionary of the Bible*, Vol. III (New York. Charles Scribner's Sons, 1900), pp. 142–143.

Index

225

Index

Index